God, Guns, & Rock'n'Roll

God, Guns, & Rock'n'Roll

BY TED NUGENT

Since 1947
REGNERY
PUBLISHING, INC.
An Eagle Publishing Company • Washington, DC

First paperback edition 2001

Library of Congress Cataloging-in-Publication Data

Nugent, Ted.
    God, guns, and rock 'n' roll / Ted Nugent.
       p. cm.
    ISBN 0-89526-173-1
      1. Gun control—United States. 2. Firearms ownership—United States. I. Title.

HV7436 .N84 2000
363.3'3'0973—dc21

00-055311

Published in the United States by
Regnery Publishing, Inc.
An Eagle Publishing Company
One Massachusetts Avenue, NW
Washington, DC 20001
www.regnery.com

Distributed to the trade by
National Book Network
4720-A Boston Way
Lanham, MD 20706

Printed on acid-free paper, by an acid-free writer
Manufactured in the United States of America

BOOK DESIGN BY MARJA WALKER

10 9 8 7 6

Books are available in quantity for promotional or premium use. Write to Director of Special Sales, Regnery Publishing, Inc., One Massachusetts Avenue, NW, Washington, DC 20001, for information on discounts and terms or call (202) 216-0600.

THIS BOOK IS DEDICATED with all my heart and soul to every brave American warrior of the U.S. Armed Forces who served and sacrificed, so "we the people" can live in what I hope is this perpetual experiment in self-government as free and sovereign beings. I dedicate this effort also to my dad, Warren Henry Nugent—one of these warriors, who taught me discipline, a hard-core work ethic, and accountability; and to my uncle John Nugent, who along with Dad introduced me to the ultimate discipline that is firearm fun: handling, responsibility, and appreciation. Also to all the dedicated warrior activists on the not-so-mean streets of this great country in the National Rifle Association, Gun Owners of America, Brass Roots, Jews for the Preservation of Firearms Ownership, and all the prohunting and pro-Second Amendment organizations across the land—especially the Ted Nugent United Sportsmen of America members who fervently fight for the basic self-evident truths and our sacred right to keep and bear arms for defense of self, family, home, and country. And to all the courageous men and women of law enforcement who commit their lives to serve and protect with the very arms that "we the people" must use to defend ourselves. And finally, this tome, like everything I do in my wonderful, adventurous, blessed life, is dedicated to my mother Marion Dorothy Nugent; brothers Jeff and John, sister Kathy, and their families; and my awe-inspiring Tribe Nuge: soulmate and wife Shemane, sons and best hunting buddies Toby and Rocco, and wonderful daughters Sasha and Starr and her family. Godbless the Tribe, Godbless America. And Godbless the attitude. 🏹

The Thin Blue Line, One Ass to Risk

"Every moving thing that liveth
shall be meat for you."

GENESIS 9:3

"Now therefore take, I pray thee,
thy weapons, thy quiver and thy bow, and go
out and take me some venison."

GENESIS 27:3

Your life starts at Point A and ends at Point B.

Kick maximum ass!

[A NOTE ON STYLE]

SOME FOLKS MIGHT REMEMBER that George Bernard Shaw—a sandal-wearing socialist vegetarian—tried to reform the spelling of the English language. Big deal. Big musty flop. This book—by the hard-drivin', hard-lovin', full-throbbin', high-octane, deerslayin', allthings-scarin', ballistic guitarboy—*Nugetizes* it. Get ready to rock, doc. ✗

[CONTENTS]

Foreword ■ *xvii*

PART 1
Cocked, Locked, and Ready to Rock, Doc

1 I'm Just a Guitar Player, But... ■ *5*

2 Walkin' Tall ■ *13*

3 The Lying Media ■ *23*

4 Denial as a Lifestyle ■ *35*

5 The Planet of the Apes ■ *43*

6 The Great Texas Machine
Gun Massacre ■ *49*

7 Gunspeak ■ *57*

8 Wanna Go to a Gun and
Knife Show? I'll Open My Jacket ■ *65*

9 BloodBrothers ■ *71*

10 We the People or We the Sheeple? ■ *81*

PART II
The Ballistics of Spirituality—
You Can't Grill It 'Til You Kill It

11 Pistolero Steakage ■ *99*

12 Rock 'n' Roll Spirit Rehab ■ *107*

13 Back to Fang ■ *117*

14 Gonzo Recipe: Celebrate the Flesh ■ *121*

15 Birdhunt Workout ■ *129*

16 Timberdoodle Dandy ■ *135*

17 Goodbye, Popeye ■ *141*

18 Texas Goose Slam ■ *145*

19 Tres Venison Hombres ■ *151*

20 The Hotbed Cradle of Man ■ *159*

21 Handgun Hunting in Africa ■ *169*

22 Shoot, Don't Shoot—The Spirit as My Guide ■ *177*

23 Outrageous Witnessed and
    Otherwise Liar Shots I Have Made ■ *183*

24 Projectile Management Marksmanship ■ *191*

PART III
Kids, Family, and the Spirit of the Wild

25 The Guitarkid and Guns ■ *201*

26 Negligent Discharges I Have Known ■ *209*

27 The White Room ■ *223*

28 Deercamp ■ *231*

29 Up North ■ *237*

30 Tribe Nuge—Giving Thanks to the Great Spirit ■ *243*

31 How to Inspire a Child into the Wild ■ *255*

32 Every Father's Dream ■ *265*

33 My Son, the Deerhunter ■ *271*

34 My Son, the Pigkiller—
    How Proud Can a Dad Get? ■ *275*

35 Guns and Kids ■ *283*

36 Nuge's Message to Kids ■ *289*

37 Fred Bear and Beyond ■ *295*

Thanx List ■ *313*
Resources ■ *316*

[FOREWORD]

IN MANY RESPECTS, Ted Nugent is a modern anachronism. As you will soon read, he believes in things and acts in ways that are of a distant past to most Americans. Make no mistake, he is not a little independent—he is a very independent person. He does things Ted's way. He thrives on intellect, self-reliance, passion, and common sense logic. He has no tolerance for people who wish to trample on or diminish his family's peaceable lifestyle.

At risk to his professional career, Ted Nugent has vociferously promoted hunting and the right to defend ourselves and our loved ones. Those of us who closely follow the hunting/shooting sports have long realized he is the only celebrity who consistently carries our message to our fellow nonhunting/nongun owning Americans. The amount of pro-hunting/Second Amendment press he has generated is staggering and unprecedented in the history of the shooting sports. Over the last ten years he has averaged at least one radio/TV/newspaper interview each day! Make a move or open your mouth to limit hunters' or gun owners' rights and you will have to deal with him. Tread on Ted at your own peril.

It would be a vast understatement to simply say that Ted Nugent enjoys guns. He cherishes them all—from BB guns to machine guns. In well-trained hands, he believes the shooting sports can provide a lifetime of enjoyment. Whether it is simply plinking with a .22 rifle or long-range handgun target shooting, Ted Nugent relishes his shooting time with his family and friends. While he is a phenomenal shot with a bow and arrow, he is even a better shot with a handgun. Gun control to Ted is putting the second bullet in the hole the first bullet made. He ardently believes that if you really want to improve a kid's hand-eye coordination, shelve the video games and put a .410 shotgun or bow and arrow in his or her hands. According to Ted, you won't find one kid in a gang with a hunter safety certificate in his back pocket.

While he clearly is astounded over how some people believe animals have rights and that America would be better off if all guns were banned, Ted Nugent is more perplexed over the lack of response from hunters and gun owners. He has often said that apathy within hunting's ranks is a cancer far worse than anything the antihunters or antigun advocates could ever hope to accomplish. He will tell you that if your elected officials don't know your name, you aren't doing enough. If you are a gun owner and aren't a member of the National Rifle Association you might as well be a card-carrying member of Handgun Control, Inc. If you hunt and don't belong to a state hunting organization and a national organization like Ted Nugent United Sportsmen of America, you are no better than antihunters.

He genuinely enjoys speaking to folks. I have seen him stop in airport terminals, grocery stores, his sons' athletic events, restaurants, etc., to talk with fellow hunters, music fans, parents, cops, and people from all walks of life. Don't expect just a quick "hello" and an autograph if he has the time. My advice if you meet Ted: pack a lunch and be prepared for some of the most engaging, entertaining conversation you have ever had. If you have your children with you, Uncle Ted always has some encouraging words for them such as socking anybody in the nose who offers them drugs or alcohol.

You should know Ted Nugent is not without his critics in the shooting sports. Some believe his message is too blunt. Others don't like that he talks about "the kill" in hunting. Still others don't like that he intersperses wit and humor into his interviews. To define his critics he often uses this analogy: A young child is being swept away in a raging river, and Ted dives in at his own peril and rescues the child from drowning. Coughing up water and nearly drowned himself, he crawls up the bank of the river with the child safely in his grasp and gives the child to the parents who then throw the child back into the river because they didn't like the way Ted swam as he rescued their child.

Seriousness aside, Ted Nugent is blessed with a tremendous sense of humor. If laughs aren't on the agenda, don't invite Ted. Throughout this book you will see that sense of humor shine through. Of the hundreds of phone calls we have shared, dozens of hunts, and time spent at his concerts, I cannot think of one of these instances where we didn't share a hearty laugh. I recall once when *Saturday Night Live* did a parody of his hunting lifestyle, many of his hunting friends were upset. Conversely, he found the skit wildly hysterical. Rarely will you see him without a huge grin on his face.

Indeed, there are only four things in life to be fearful of: a coiled rattlesnake, a grizzly sow with cubs, a charging cape buffalo, and Ted Nugent in the left lane in a rent-a-car.

Enjoy the book. Welcome to Full Bluntal Nugety.

—WARD PARKER
National Director's Chairman
Ted Nugent United Sportsmen of America
Summer 2000

PART 1
COCKED, LOCKED, AND
READY TO ROCK, DOC

A strong body makes the mind strong. As to the species of exercises, I advise the gun. While this gives moderate exercise to the body, it gives boldness, enterprise and independence to the mind. Games played with the ball, and others of that nature, are too violent for the body and stamp no character on the mind. Let your gun, therefore, be the constant companion of your walks.

THOMAS JEFFERSON

Firearms stand next in importance to the Constitution itself. They are the American people's liberty teeth and keystone under independence.... From the hour the pilgrims landed, to the present day events, occurrences and tendencies prove that to insure peace, security and happiness, the rifle and pistol are equally indispensable.... The very atmosphere of firearms everywhere restrains evil interference—they deserve a place of honor with all that's good.

GEORGE WASHINGTON

Had America continued with the quality control of disciplined gun safety education as did our forefathers up through the 1960s, coupled with commonsense law enforcement and a justice system that recognizes something resembling justice, we would not have to be scrambling for such apparent damage control now.

TED NUGENT

When in doubt, whip it out.

NUGE

CHAPTER 1

I'M JUST A GUITAR PLAYER, BUT...

SCREECHING TIRES SCREAMED in my right ear as burning rubber erupted just outside my open taxicab window, and I instinctively recoiled and spun to see the cause. The green Chevy shortbed pickup truck's off-road suspension rocked and rolled as it stopped and angled sharply across the congested rush hour traffic lanes of Collins Avenue. Stinking, rubbery, blue smoke billowed from the extended wheel wells of the still bucking half-ton. Immediately, two shirtless, muscled men catapulted from the cab, leaping up and over the tool-filled bed, yelling outrage at the

> Only a coward would want fewer good guys with guns on the streets in today's world. Only a fool would support— much less design— such a policy of helplessness.

occupant of the small, silver Japanese car they had just cut off. A tall, young, dark-haired Cuban-looking man unfolded his lanky frame from the cornered vehicle, and my eyes zeroed in on the black fanny pouch he wore slightly off center at his waist.

Just moments before, easing into a wonderful night with my lovely wife Shemane, I had been in standard "Condition Yellow." That is a state of relaxed awareness, a condition one trains to maintain so as to be not just cognizant of one's surroundings, but ultimately prepared for the unexpected. Now, I was jolted instantly past phase two of my training, Condition Orange, and headfirst into full-blown Condition Red. Knowing of the recent dramatic increase in concealed weapon permits issued here in South Florida, I instantly thought "GUN!" My tactical law enforcement training kicked in.

Powerful, soul-driving instincts came alive and, with my left hand, I swung open the left, curbside door, shoving my precious wife to cover behind the only bullet-stopping shield available—the rear wheel of our gridlocked cab. At once my right hand flipped open my cell phone and I punched #1, speed dialing 911. I yelled intensely to the taxi driver to get down as the dispatch operator came on. My eyes clicked to eagle mode and peered intently at the escalating clash as the two muscular attackers bowled over their target with violent force.

Slammed to the concrete and already bloody, the overwhelmed young man somehow thrust both hands into his belt pouch as fist after fist nailed his head and upper torso with machine gun–like repetition. I figured, "This is it, here comes the gun." But instead of producing just a gun, he flailingly yanked both a gun and a police badge at once. Knowing all too well the statistics of cops being slain with their own guns (one in six), my fear and awareness intensified and went into overdrive, proportionate to the escalating confrontation before me.

Clueless, sheep-like citizens were now gathering around the bloody fisticuffs, gawking as if it were a cockfight. Meanwhile, a stainless .357 magnum was wildly whipping about, as the off-duty Dade County policeman was struggling to control his revolver and fighting for his life. Bloody fists were flying like mad dog, muscle-driven pile-drivers—the skinny cop was bloody, his shirt pulled up over his head, and he was being thrown about the pavement like a rag doll by the powerful duo.

Maybe two or three seconds had transpired thus far when I responded to the 911 operator, overemphasizing my diction and resolve to deliver the urgency and clear details of my potentially lifesaving message: "A PLAINCLOTHES POLICE OFFICER IS BEING ASSAULTED BY TWO SHIRTLESS CAUCASIAN MEN ON THE EAST CURBSIDE OF NORTH-

BOUND COLLINS AVENUE AT THE ROYAL HOTEL DRIVEWAY. THEY ARE FIGHTING FOR THE POLICEMAN'S GUN. MY NAME IS TED NUGENT, AND I AM A SPECIAL DEPUTY FROM GENESSEE COUNTY, MICHIGAN. I AM SIX FOOT TWO, CAUCASIAN, WEARING SHORTS, A YELLOW SLEEVELESS SHIRT, I HAVE A LONG PONYTAIL, I AM ARMED AND GOING IN TO HELP THE OFFICER. SEND POLICE AND AN AMBULANCE IMMEDIATELY."

In nonstop motion I flipped my Motorola cell phone shut, instructed Shemane to stay behind the wheel beside the cab, pocketed my phone, made sure my Glock Model 20, 10mm handgun was clear and forward on my right hip for optimum access, whipped open my sheriff's badge in my left hand, and charged forcefully into the melee like a mother grizzly sow protecting her cubs. I could taste rage, fear, blood, and terror. I was 190 pounds of broiling adrenaline. All systems, 100 PERCENT, DUMP NOW! Full Bluntal Nugety. The MotorCity Madman in his prime. Somewhere inside me a prayer gushed forth.

My vision was a laser beam, and I distinctly saw only the three players in a tunnel surrounded by haze; my eyes riveted on the spinning silver handgun. My mindset was ridiculously clear. If the two assailants got control of the cop's gun, I would be ready and obligated to use my law enforcement training in the use of deadly force to neutralize the threat and save the officer's life and other innocent lives. So with flamethrowing eye-balls wider and wilder than my *Cat Scratch Fever* album cover photo, crazy-ass rock 'n' roll hair flying, and my loudest, most insane Double Live Gonzo spit enhanced screams, I yelled at the top of my petrified lungs, "STOP, POLICE! GET THE FUCK BACK, POLICE!!!," nearly shoving my badge clean through the face of the closest guy. To my utter astonishment and relief, both perpe-trators actually ceased their aggres-sion, let go of the cop, put up their hands, and backed away from their fallen, bloody victim.

> Criminals celebrate when politicians clear the path for their destructive ways.

At that moment a covey of uniformed officers con-verged on the scene from all directions, both on foot and in patrol cars, like angry killer bees and immediately and conclusively took control. Luckily, my gold sheriff deputy shield identified me readily as a good guy, for the responding officers had guns drawn, pointing at all of our faces, eyes afire, thus escalating my fear a few more notches into the stratosphere. I was beyond uncool. At any moment I would surely turn into a puddle of foam-ing piss and hair. All responding officers were wildly aggressive with the two perps, slamming them violently onto the hoods of the patrol cars, three on one. They handcuffed them and shoved them into the police cars. A virtual whitewater rapids of adrenaline still ran amok.

I stuck around just long enough to give a long, hyperventilated, and detailed statement to one of the officers. Then Shemane and I celebrated our tenth anniversary as calmly and enjoyably as could be expected after such an intense adrenaline-infested experience. My head verily spun with the possibilities that might have been. Certainly, if it were not for the gun in my belt, law enforcement training, instantaneous decision-making awareness, and attitude to do the right thing, there is no way in hell I would have ever gotten involved in such an outright deadly dangerous situation. But I did, I do, and I will. I could do it because I had the necessary tool for the job at hand. My primary instinct and drive to survive dictated all my actions. Without a means to defend—without the Glock loaded and ready with sixteen rounds of Cor-Bon ammo riding ever ready in my Galco holster—I would have been as helpless as the rest of the defenseless public standing by without a clue. To my mind, it is wholly irresponsible to go into the world incapable of preventing violence, injury, crime, and death. How feeble is the mindset to accept defenselessness. How unnatural. How cheap. How cowardly. How pathetic.

Only a coward would want fewer good guys with guns on the streets in today's world. Only a fool would support—much less design—such a policy of helplessness. When President Bill Clinton lies about putting 100,000 new cops on the streets, but refuses to allow millions of dedicated, trained law enforcement and licensed citizen warriors to carry their guns legally across the country, the writing is on the wall. In Congress, House Resolution 218—Community Protection Act—would remedy this foolish situation, but Al Gore, Bill Clinton, Sarah Brady, Janet Reno, Charlie Schumer, Bill Bradley, Dianne Feinstein, and their antihuman ilk will have none of it thank you. Criminals celebrate when politicians clear the path for their destructive ways.

The options for me that day were blatantly obvious: (1) stand around like the other helpless souls and stare, (2) hide and whimper, (3) run, or (4) put a halt to the unacceptable situation, neutralize the violence, and save innocent lives. The only way possible is with a warrior attitude and a gun. Any questions? Dial 1-800-NUMBNUT. Next.

CHAPTER 2

WALKIN' TALL

EVERY DAY SINCE 1 LEFT home after graduating from high school in 1967 at the tender age of eighteen, I have instinctively taken my independence seriously. As a matter of practice I have stuffed my pockets with simple yet specific urban survival gear: a clean handkerchief, a pocketknife, a wad of thin guitar picks, my wallet with some cash and ID, and a handful of ammo. The attitude came naturally, too. Snugged into my belt in the small of my back went a silver 2-inch roundbutt Smith & Wesson Model 19, .357 magnum revolver. I wouldn't have it any

Drugs and alcohol destroy one's level of awareness sure as hell. This is not an opinion. It is a self-evident truth 1 thought 1 would pass along for the benefit of those not paying attention.

other way. I didn't give it a ton of thought. It just seemed like the right thing to do. Be prepared. The alternative would be to flounder like a weenie. I'd rather stand up next to the mountain and chop it down with the edge of my hand.

Surrounded by stoned hippies preaching peace and love like so many lost souls, I stood tall, different, cocked, locked, and ready to rock. For the life of me I could not imagine the intellectual bankruptcy that would allow anyone to intentionally pursue a reduced level of awareness, much less accept total defenselessness. I lived in the shadows of Detroit City, for God's sake. What kind of spineless dolt would dare venture forth virtually incapable of wiping his or her nose or surviving the vicious predator mentality of the paroled masses on the planet of the apes? Not I, sayeth the guitarboy. Want my car? Come and get it, Cornelius.

And the pressure was intense.

I was always different. Nobody understood. I
didn't play Follow the Leader, cuz I was always
in the woods. They hadn't invented peer pressure yet, it seemed I stood alone. But my daddy
had a vision—love, family, and a home. Punks
used to laugh at me, they said, how can ya rock

and not get high? So I just stood my ground,
and I watched those assholes fall and die.

That's a lyric from my huntsong, "I Just Wanna Go Huntin'," and it's accurate. Though I was certainly blessed and deeply appreciative to connect with many dedicated virtuoso musicians early on, beyond our musical relationship nothing else about our lifestyles or ideologies related in any way, shape, or form. I could not have been more different. Makes me think of a song title, "You Talk Sunshine, I Shit Napalm." Of course, it would have to be a lovesong. I not only turned down dope from my fellow musicians and friends, I actually was defiant enough to refuse the lube of trendy chemicals from the adventurous silken hands of dynamo-humbabes. En masse. On the eternal prowl. Looking for guitarlove. I craved getting laid beyond the best of 'em, but not if it meant destroying my level of awareness or compromising my senses and drooling. Not only that, but all the hippie chicks had crabs. I was looking for the special ones. You know, those that put value on personal hygiene. I don't need no fancy types; I needs the ones that's clean, hey baby.

If I remember correctly—and being free of poisons for fifty-two years, I do—it was around '59 that I invented the middle finger. Not just any middle finger, mind you, but a specialized SWAT, throbbing, bulbous, gut-ridden, dirty-nailed middle digit of intense defiance. Unlike the hipsters with their vacuous "rebel without a cause" bullshit, I had a major cause called quality of independent life. I was Rosa Parks with a loud guitar. And the lovely silver gun hidden in my belt during the outlando drug-infested hippie years went undetected and unexposed. I saved my total uninhibitedness for guitartime. America can thank its lucky stars that I didn't get stoned. I would have shot everybody. Might not have been a bad idea. Of course, I didn't have to, because plenty of them killed themselves in the name of hip. Hey, I got a good idea, let's go to a jam session tonight and celebrate the spirited, creative overjuiceflow of Jimi Hendrix, Keith Moon, Mike Bloomfield, Brian Jones, Phil Lynott, Dennis Wilson, Bon Scott, John Belushi, Janis Joplin, Jim Morrison, Jerry Garcia, and a stupifyingly long list of the hippest idiots that ever lived. And died. Would if we could, but Jimi got high and Jimi's dead, I went huntin' and I'm still Ted. And I was the fool, right? They all laughed at me because I wouldn't indulge in their feeble drug and booze games. The one time Jimi saw my gun, he thought I was way out there. Now they ain't got no life nowhere. 'Scuse me whilst I kiss the sky.

And the peacenicks wouldn't just offer me drugs, they would get nasty and belligerent—often violent.

They were dumbfounded that the energized, out of control wildman with the unleashed, mastadon-mating, roaring, feedback guitar would actually say no to the groovy drug of the week. But I did more than just say no. Oh yeah, I did. I busted more hippies' noses than all the narcboys in the free world. There were times I would have to punch my way out of a room because these imbeciles would get physical and try to force joints and cocaine and shit into my face.

Like one night down in Huntsville, Alabama, around '69, some typically dirty, smelly, booger-ridden hippie goofball in a mustard-stained Grateful Dead, nasty-ass, roadkill-smelling-like-hell ragshirt really got pushy with his vial of coke. He was absolutely incredulous that his hero, The MotorCity Madman, would actually turn down his blow. This jerk couldn't comprehend my declining on sheer principle. To him, that was just inconceivable. He thought I was turning down his personal peace offering, and he got deeply offended and noisy, his fragile, tofu-driven senses being crushed, dontchya know. Of course, the middle finger within Young Ted went ballistic when he started pushing and shoving. And remember, when I use the word ballistic, I take the lovely term to heart. I merely pretended to acquiesce, took his shit, and lured him into the nearest bathroom where I proceeded to flush his sacred poison down the toilet. He went mentally berserk, what can best be described as an accidental or negligent pineal discharge, and lunged for me and his precious escape drugs. At which point, I slammed his face into the bowl along with the coke, then dragged him out into the backstage hallway where I threw him at the feet of some young security officer, who I hope had his nightstick way with the turd. I never asked. If only we had vidcams then. You'd want a copy.

But I also never pulled my gun. It would have been total overkill—which has a nice ring to it, but I wouldn't dare. I value my freedom deeply. And there are empirical laws of the jungle. The truism of tooth, fang, and claw has a certain, unmovable, immemorial honor that must be upheld. One who carries a gun can never get into a pissing match with the fleebs. A gunboy must remain above that pit of pettiness. Feelings be damned; it's lives we wish to save.

This hippie dippie drugnut nonsense went undeterred everywhere I toured throughout the '60s, '70s, and well into the '80s. Hell, even into the '90s for God's sake. Astonishingly enough, I am aware that it still goes on today, though the participating pukes avoid me, America's #1 narc rocker, like the plague. It saddens me immensely, not just that the vast majority of musicians and entertainers who receive the majority of media coverage are viciously antigun and antihunting, but more so that the typical anti is more than willing to tolerate or indulge in—and therefore encourage—the insanity of drugs. *I would like to repeat an important announcement I have been screaming nonstop for thirty years—**the drug experiment is over, and Victoria has no secrets!** See that mudhole over yonder, kids? See all the crippled folk drooling in their wheelchairs? See the tubes attached? They failed to check the water's depth a long time ago, and all these paralyzed people dove in anyway. They all broke their necks, cantchya see? Read that huge neon sign over there. It says:* THE WATER'S NOT DEEP ENOUGH! IF YOU DIVE IN LIKE THEY DID, YOU WILL BE PARALYZED TOO! Which part don't they get?

Drugs and alcohol destroy one's level of awareness sure as hell. This is not an opinion. It is a self-evident truth I thought I would pass along for the benefit of those not paying attention. And I beseech each and every one out there who gives a good goddamn about quality of life to spread this good word far and wide. Intolerance would be a step in the right direction. Please. Good Lord!

To see monstrously talented bands like the Red Hot Chili Peppers, in the 1990s for God's sake, destroy themselves with drugs and even heroin is mind-boggling to say the least. Thank God they've survived and cleaned up. Most of these mind-altered bands would leap at the chance to help with an antigun benefit, but wallow in denial that drug and alcohol abuse slaughter a thousand times as many innocent lives as all gunplay combined. Go figure.

And don't believe for a minute the wild-ass lies of their stoned leaders like Jann Wenner of "Rolling Stoned" magazine. As head honcho of Cease Fire, this goofball blatantly manipulates and controls the words and pages of his powerful publications under the bullet-proof umbrella of the First Amendment while he laughs out loud wiping his ass with the Second. Though oft repeated in rags like his, a handgun IS NOT forty-seven times more likely to kill a family member, unless of course, you and the whole tribe are in the crack runnin' trade and/or on parole as a lifestyle. That ramrod figure is as false as Jann's wedding vows. After he left his wife and children to go off into the sunset, ass in hand, with his new boyfriend, he turned up his antigun heat by increasing his hateful editorials and free magazine ad space with outrageous twisted lies about guns and gun owners.

Meanwhile, the government's own statistics prove overwhelmingly that since the various Clinton gun-bans, the resulting huge and unprecedented increase in gun ownership and concealed weapons permits nation-wide has America experiencing the lowest violent crime rate, including gun crimes, in more than forty years. John Lott, Jr., senior research scholar at Yale Law School, and David Mustard, economist at the University of Georgia, concluded with their eighteen-year scientific study and Lott's book *More Guns, Less Crime* that, indeed, more guns, less crime *is* truly common sense. Those who wish to disarm America hate to admit it, but the FBI, Bureau of Alcohol, Tobacco, and Firearms (BATF), National Shooting Sports Foundation, Center for Disease Control, and all national crime studies substantiate this conclusion. And how tough is it to grasp that when the law disarms good guys, bad guys rejoice? Why haven't Sam Donaldson, Tom Brokaw, Dan Rather, et. al. mentioned that recently? Statistically, for every round fired in the commission of a crime, literally *trillions* are fired legally, safely, and properly. That's a trillion to one!

[CHAPTER 3]

THE LYING MEDIA

I'VE KNOWN IT FOREVER, and Jesse Ventura figured it out pretty quick. The vast majority of America's free press does not report news, they make it up. Anyone who dismisses the claims of a conspiracy is either a paid employee of the media or a deaf, dumb, and blind fool. Especially dumb. Though the examples are too numerous to list, one of my favorites is the number of times I have watched a network newscast on crime. I cannot count the instances I have witnessed where a violent assault or murder was being "reported," and though the crime was already determined to have been committed with a pipe, bat, knife, club, or hatchet, there was that ever present graphic of a handgun shown in maximum size on the TV screen right next to the oh-so-compassionate anchorhead's face. The power of repetitious imagery is the ultimate propaganda. They know it and continue it intentionally.

There was the time around 1996 when an overly creative pop music critic of a Texas newspaper wrote his review of my sold-out concert at the Starplex Amphitheater. Being forty-seven years clean and sober at the time, my observations from the stage that night, like every night, are the most accurate to be had, bias be damned. I feed and thrive on these eagle-eye, face-to-face observations in order to custom tune my set and performance to suck maximum positive exuberance from the workin' hard, playin' hard supporters in attendance over all these years and deliver to them the absolute best rockout I possibly can for their hard-earned money. I take this long-running relationship very, very seriously.

This particular concert was an undeniable musical escapade for my band. We went where no whites have gone before on a musical, emotional, sonic bombast, cerebral, intestinal, sexual, sensual, predator, primal scream, soul of man, and spiritual level. It was nothing short of a damn middle finger lovefest. Michael Cartellone on drums and Michael Lutz on the bass guitar were sensational, inspired. These guys work themselves into a lather, they put so much heart and soul into their performances. They are the gruesome twosome of high velocity rhythm and blues. Absolute monster virtuosos.

This evening we were as tight on as our heroes James Brown and his Famous Flames. We are always intensely motivated to kill ourselves for every audience every night out of sheer pride in musicianship and the musical escapade we create. We give it all we got. I invented and perfected Hi-Energy rock 'n' roll. The outrageous energy, tightness, cohesiveness, passion, outright piss and vinegar we produced this night was truly special. After all, we were in the land of Stevie Ray Vaughn, ZZ Top, and the powerful history of guitar slingers *par excellence* on which Texas had been spoiled. My enthusiasm was at a frightening high. The crowd was on its feet the entire ninety minutes, and the unanimous dancing, cheering, roaring, smiling response throughout the set was undeniable. Unless of course you were a renowned ultra-liberal, gun-hating, NRA-bashing, hunting-despising, Nugent-slamming, stoned trendgeek of a pop music critic, that is.

Now, mind you, if you are antigun and antihunter in your politics, there is plenty about Uncle Ted to criticize, even hate, without looking too hard. There should be no reason to lie. But I have always brought out the best in people, especially frustrated Grateful Dead fans like that ol' pop critic. They cannot stand that I have been selling out concerts in Texas for more than thirty-three years, still holding many attendance records there with guaranteed standing ovations every night, making all my own decisions, being my own boss, and celebrating Full Bluntal Nugety with relentless aplomb. So in his tortured frustration he resorted to lying. He claimed ol' Nuge was "plodding" and "lifeless." Well, there ya have it, kids. Accurate, honest, descriptive words if there were any to describe what it is I do with my guitar. He referenced specifically the "lifeless" version of my lovesong, "DOG EAT DOG" from the alleged "plodding" performance that night. The beauty of his wonderful writing style is that on that particular night, "DOG EAT DOG" was in fact NOT performed at all. Not a good version or a bad version. No version. It was not on the setlist. Hello? He also went into a vicious diatribe in his pop critic column on how I "ranted all night about the NRA and guns in general." But I didn't mention the word "guns" even once that night, as any tape recording of the show proves. Meanwhile, this inept, dishonest, unprofessional "journalist" continues to have unobstructed delivery of his misinformation to the public. Truth? He don't care 'bout no stinkin' truth. The boy got agenda.

CBS got agenda, too, as it proved when it produced a deliberate fraud on one of its twisted gun specials. In this particular episode of CBS's *48 Hours*, they cleverly edited footage of a standard, legal semi-automatic rifle, supposedly being converted to full auto within nine short minutes. Much to their journalistic suicide, the machine gun they showed on TV at the end of the so called "conversion" was a completely different arm altogether. An expert from the BATF later said that the claimed conversion was virtually impossible.

On Denver's KMGH-TV, a reporter railed on the evils of "assault weapons," showing footage of people firing fully automatic machine guns. He claimed they were semi-auto "assault weapons" that needed to be banned (already were!). Good work all you highly trained, believable professionals. We salute you for your integrity in time of need. Such depth.

The execs at big media know exactly what they are doing. Remember the tragedy in Pearl, Mississippi, where two students were murdered and seven injured by a boy named Luke Woodham? Little reported was the fact that his rampage was halted by Joel Myrick, for the simple and singular reason that this teacher had a .45 pistol in his car, handy enough to bring into play and save lives. Woodham had more ammo and admitted he was intent on killing all he could. Solidly sticking to their malicious MO, the network news almost entirely ignored the fact that it was an armed teacher who stopped him.

Brian Patrick, a University of Michigan communications researcher and author of *The National Rifle Association and the Media: The Motivating Force of Negative Coverage,* quotes the chairman of the Media Research Center, Brent Bozell, as saying, "It's clear that when it comes to the gun debate, TV news is no objective referee. It is a partisan player that has chosen sides— the anti-gun, anti-Second Amendment side."

A Media Research Center study determined that between July 1997 and July 1999, of 653 gun-related stories on ABC, CBS, NBC, and CNN, reports advocating gun control outnumbered stories opposing gun control by 357 to 36, a ratio of almost ten to one.

Much of the media is spreading another big lie with outrageous claims that the police agencies of America are "outgunned." Balderdash! Pure unadulterated bullshit. There is no law enforcement agency in America that doesn't have immediate access to military-style firepower. MP5 submachine guns, M16s, maximum capacity riot 12-gauge shotguns, sniper rifles—you name it, most got it. And if I hear one more reporter misidentify a 9mm handgun as an "assault pistol" or a "high-powered" handgun, I think I'm gonna pee myself. The 9mm is better than a sharp stick, but not by much. I consider it a minimum defense round and better suited for small game like rabbits and squirrels. For practical purposes, there is no standard handgun round that qualifies as "high-powered." Even the venerable .44 magnum is a pipsqueak compared to almost any long gun round, about par with the historical 30-30 Winchester.

The examples of fraud, manipulation, twisted statistics, and out and out lies about guns by the media are unlimited. But the mother of all media lies came from that illegitimate toxic mongrel Michael Gartner, former president of NBC. He's the bubba who "executive produced" the classic NBC special on GM pickup truck gas-tank explosions. Unfortunately for Mikey, he got caught letting a pyrotechnician blow up the truck. His truck "collision" was staged. His special "documentary" was, in fact, a fraud. That fraud was nothing compared to his famous gun special. You see, Mikey is on public record stating his official personal gun policy. He and his communist ilk support Fidel Castro's totalitarian gun policy where "only military and police should have any access to any firearms whatsoever." That of course was Adolf's, Idi's, and Pol Pot's system. Meanwhile, with total control over what is delivered as a "news report," Gartnerboy constructed a feature presentation loaded with lie after lie after lie. The claim repeated over and

> **The examples of fraud, manipulation, twisted statistics, and out and out lies about guns by the media are unlimited.**

over again—that a gun in the house is forty-seven times more likely to be used against someone you know—is laughable, at best. That oft-parroted nonsense is a manufactured stat derived from a Handgun Control, Inc., report. The stat comes from examining shootings and discovering that those involved actually knew each other... as in dope dealer and buyer, dope runner and supplier, Crips shooting the Bloods, pimps shooting their whores, domestic violence convicts who are out of jail to shoot their honey *again*! That kind of stupidity. What the hell that has to do with the hundreds of millions of gun owners who do not shoot each other evades me. I wrote a song titled KLSTRPHK that pretty well describes what Michael Gartner and the majority of major media in America are up to when it comes to reporting the news.

Can any of us ever forget or clear our minds from the relentless pummeling by the major media, especially the networks, as they seemed to celebrate the outrageous criminal shooting episodes over the last few years? The sensational headlines and leading stories of ol' early-paroled, fumbling alleged murderer Buford Furrow hosing down the little children at the Los Angeles area Jewish day care center with his semi-auto 9mm Uzi seemed to never end. The Uzi (which by California law has been banned for years, and of course all felons are forbidden from possessing any firearm) got top billing most of the time with almost no mention of Buford's early release or the judge or parole board who made that well thought out decision. And how could it be that with the devastating killing efficiency of an *Uzi*, no one was killed? Meanwhile, a short few weeks later, a maniac in a Cadillac intentionally ran over a playground full of children not far from the same area, killing six and severely injuring more than a dozen. And I ask you, where was that story? I'll tell you where it was: it was buried. My logic concludes that the conspiratorial media monsters don't give a rat's ass about dead kids, they are simply consumed with guns. Their gun-banning agenda completely overshadows their concern for dead kids, a corrupt justice system, braindead judges, accurate reporting, or anything resembling ethical journalism. But I'm just a guitar player, what do I know?

As my last example of manipulative journalism, I give you the hysterical VH-1 *Behind the Music* specials. Now, I am not so sure that the producers have actually delivered what might be called fraud or intentional misrepresentation in the standard production technique of these highly successful specials, but the unprecedented approach they customized for my *Ted Nugent: Behind the Music* episode tells us much about the depth of bias that exists in all factions of the media when it comes to

guns and hunting—especially their special treatment of
that lone someone who has continually stood up for
guns and hunting within their own entertainment industry. They must not like that at all.

As feature after feature on the careers of artist after
artist runs across the TV screen, we witness a runaway
epidemic of death, destruction, crime, drug abuse,
viciousness, demonic worship, self-mutilation, drinking
and driving, puking, violence, murder, rape, suicide,
child abuse, and on and on to a putrid level. Every damn
rock band like so many mindless sheep indulging in the
same imbecilic stupidity like clockwork. Meanwhile, ol'
Ted's special is the only one ever to have a disclaimer
during the intro or to have invited commentary by
people who in no way had ever had anything to do with
my career. And it just so happens that those chosen to
comment on me were avowed animal rights and/or
extreme antigun activists. Seeing as how I have never in
my life partaken in the bullshit of drugs, alcohol abuse, or
crime, all my *Behind the Music* special exposed about me
was that I was a hunter and NRA board member. How
dare I stand up for my God-given rights as guaranteed
by the U.S. Constitution or the truth? Meanwhile all the
sheeprockers with AIDS, heroin and methadone addic-
tion, runaway substance abuse, and criminal inclina-
tions are treated like poor innocent victims at least, and

at times, real life heroes of the rock world. Perfectly understandable journalism, if you live on the planet of the apes. ✗

CHAPTER 4

DENIAL AS A LIFESTYLE

OF COURSE THIS BRINGS us to what I believe to be the most important chapter in this book and, I believe, in any family's life: accepting the fact that everybody, especially kids, are at the very least interested in guns and more often than not absolutely fascinated with them. The attraction of firearms, for a myriad of reasons, is a

There's this little ditty I discovered in the wilds of nature that we as a society desperately need to get back to: it's called cause and effect.

powerful force in people's lives. Always has been and always will be. Get over it. Most important, do something smart about it.

Something about guns—their fascinating and romantic history, mechanical and aesthetic beauty, the shooting fun, firepower, the marksmanship challenge, their unique lifesaving properties, and their mystical charisma—create one hell of an attractant. Knowing and accepting this to be true, the simple and intelligent response is to initiate a gun dialogue with family members, especially children. The very worst thing anyone could do is attempt to dismiss or deny them or back off. With outrageously sensationalized gun imagery everywhere we look in the entertainment world—from cartoons to nearly every damn movie and TV show, contemporary music, videos, *ad nauseum*—we as a society have glorified the gun beyond anyone's wildest imagination. With that reality driving a much more honest and responsible response, parents must come to grips with the blatant and totally unnecessary history of negligence and rule-breaking if we are to realistically address and ultimately remedy this issue. Though the statistics once again clearly show that kids killed by guns are way down on the list of accidental deaths, lives can and must be saved.

The very same goes for drugs, booze, drinking and driving, unprotected sex, unwanted pregnancies, plastic bags, diving into untested shallow ponds, junk food, dull knives, wild animals, powertools, cleaning solvents, loud guitars, the middle finger, and fire. The list is endless. Subjects unexplored are areas of increased risk of danger and mistake-making. Nowhere near enough serious scrutiny is given these subjects by parents with their children, and I for one have made it a communication regimen at the Nuge household. We talk about everything in all the uninhibited, gory detail we can muster. Nothing should be sacred and no subject off-limits. A gangrenous appendage unattended to will kill you sure as hell. Face it, accept the discomfort and pain, lop the damn thing off, and save your life. Move on.

At the very least, every family desperately needs to upgrade their overall communication program on every subject, guns notwithstanding. A wonderful first step to reuniting the American family, and thereby upgrading the state of the nation, would be to reestablish the family meal regimen. Rare are the families who gather at the traditional dinner table to share meals and insight into each other's lives and experiences. The movie *American Beauty* was sad because it reminds us of the ever expanding spiritual chasm between bloodkin. Isn't it pathetic that a family can live in the same house, living and eating side by side, but not really know each other at all? Is junior sawing off shotguns in his room?

Isn't it clear how horrible this situation has gotten when we witness the epidemic of obesity in America while wimpy family members cannot bring themselves to intervene even when they see the vulgar explosion of blubber gobbling up the ones they claim to love? I'd like to see less worry about hurting feelings and start actually saving lives. After all, the number one cause of premature death in America today isn't gun-related, it is *diet*-related. We are not talking subtle weight gain by brother and sis. We're talking rotund, gargantuan, blubber-infested monsters amongst us. Take a look at yourself and your kids naked as they get out of the bathtub. What do you see? Can you hide a fist or maybe the lawn mower in their gut? Do they wear huge T-shirts at the beach and swimming pool? Are they teased for being fat? Is all this necessary? No, not in a million years. They're obese. Help them. Take away the cookies and pop now. Speak up and show some real love. If we tolerate such outrageously unhealthy visible conditions on their outside, what are we allowing to fester inside?

> There is a simple answer to crime. It's called enforcing the law.

When six-year-old crack babies from the planet of the apes shoot a fellow kindergartner, the writing is on the wall—in blood. And what is the planet of the apes? It is inhabited by a different species than that which I belong to, that's for damn sure. It is where state social workers, neighbors, families, and everyone—in plain view of recidivistic, outrageous criminals—ignore the blaring sirens and accept violence, drugs, and lawlessness as a way of life. It's where apathy is on a stampede. In this particular American horror story, teachers actually caught the kid with a knife—the very day he gunned down the other child. Nothing was done, of course. His dad was in prison, his mother on parole, his aunts and uncles all crack monsters, and the authorities knew it. And the apes scratched their ass in confusion. Brilliant. There's this little ditty I discovered in the wilds of nature that we as a society desperately need to get back to: it's called cause and effect. You either get it or it gets you. Admit to that answer and get crackin', quick.

If we were to honestly review the years leading up to the tragic school shootings of the '90s—Jonesboro, Springfield, Edinborough, Pearl, Columbine, and Flint—we would clearly see a pattern of hopeless disassociation by a bunch of isolated, fragmented moms, dads, brothers, and sisters who didn't have the faintest idea what each other's daily lives or minds consisted of. And don't think for a minute that a fleeting wave, a spiritless kiss, and a heartless hug with the cursory "How was school today?" or a feeble "How was your day?" accomplishes jacksquat. Caring parents belong in conversation, at the dinner table, in the livingroom, in the woods, with their kids—all the time.

In my own rural Michigan community, I received a desperate phone call from my chief of police when these school crimes were becoming rampant. My son's public school had received a threatening Internet message and a letter. Our dedicated police chief was intent that the pattern of death and destruction wouldn't be repeated here. So the chief acted immediately. The individual responsible for the threats was in custody, but it was uncertain if others were involved. I was proud to assist, as the chief asked me to, in orchestrating a school assembly where I did a Drug Abuse Resistance Education (DARE) presentation—armed, of course—preaching the gospel against drugs and violence, and encouraging awareness of potential danger. We covered all bases with undercover officers and a well-orchestrated plan. Happily, nothing happened at our school because of an aggressive screening process for troublemakers, and by the disciplined professionalism of local teachers and law enforcement.

But the astonishing reaction we got from the parents of the sixteen-year-old author of the school threats is a perfect example of the absurd denial and mindless parenting at the heart of youth violence and crime in America today. When confronted with the irrefutable evidence of their son's death threat to certain students, the pathetic parents refused to read the Internet threat or the letter without first getting their son's permission. They made some outrageous claim that it would be wrong for them to "snoop" or "pry" or otherwise breech the boy's privacy. Get that. This shameless parental wimpout would be bad enough under any conditions, but out and out aiding and abetting in the current state of youth violence *modus operandi*? Snoop? Pry? I got news for everybody out there: Prying and snooping is the moral obligation of parenting where I come from. Jailtime should be the very minimum this brat should receive, but like the six thousand kids caught with guns in school from 1996 through 1998, the justice system did nothing. Nothing except send a voluminous message to all kids that felonies with guns are A–OK, not to worry. This failure to enforce felony statutes that on paper demand a minimum sentence is what helps young criminals think they can get away with it—again and again. Recidivism by rote. Apathy is curse one in America. Lop it off.

And as my Ted Nugent United Sportsmen of America buddy reminded some folks yesterday, denial ain't a river in Egypt. But the mind-bogglingly gruesome level of denial in the Special Olympics we call politics was manifest again in another recent crime. At the National Zoo (how appropriate) in Washington, D.C., it appears by all eyewitness accounts that a gang of youngsters had gathered and argued. I certainly hope no feelings were hurt. One such youngster, a black male between fifteen and seventeen years of age (Am I profiling here?), must have taken exception at the escalating argument and decided to start shooting. That's all ugly enough. But Connecticut Senator Christopher Dodd didn't help when, in a televised statement, he proudly, self-righteously plummeted way down into new, exciting uncharted depths of denial. He had the outrageous audacity to say that this shooting proves we need more gun laws, actually citing a specific need for trigger locks! May I? (1) People under eighteen are forbidden from owning or possessing handguns. (2) All firearms are banned in Washington, D.C. (3) Discharging a firearm in the city limits is against the law. (4) Shooting at people is illegal. (5) Could any serious-thinking person think that gunlocks prevent gang-bang wars? Take President Clinton's recent claim: "I'm not at all sure that even a callous, irresponsible drug dealer with a six-year-old kid in the house wouldn't leave a child trigger lock on a gun." REALLY? Are these politicians members of the same species that I am?

There is a simple answer to crime. It's called enforcing the law. Remind your elected representative about that the next time he wants to restrict *your* rights rather than simply put the bad guys in the slammer. Dodd and Clinton: my nominees for co-mayors of the planet of the apes. ⚔

[CHAPTER 5]

THE PLANET OF THE APES

LET ME GET THIS STRAIGHT: The sheeping of
Running, crying, whimpering, and America is nearly
hiding under desks and pews? You complete.
mean to say that when an imbecile
walks into a church, office, day care center, or school,
stumbling about, almost zombie-like, with gun-filled
hands at his side, blabbering incoherently to his next
victim, the reaction of grown men and women is to run,
cry, whimper, and hide under a desk or pew? The
sheeping of America is nearly complete.

When George Hennard drove his pickup truck
through the window of Luby's cafeteria in Killeen,
Texas years ago, most of his victims cowered beneath
dining tables, blubbering—except for one brave warrior,

Al Gratia, who, though unarmed by law, still bravely attempted to stop the madman and was murdered in the process. He and his wife were two of the twenty-three slaughtered that day. You see, by Texas law, they were unarmed and defenseless. Meanwhile, the murderer actually squatted with his back to people as he casually explained why he would kill his next victim. He would have been ridiculously easy to stop before he killed again if someone would have been armed. In fact, he was so nonchalant about his actions it would have been a simple matter of breaking a damn chair over his head.

In Buckhead, Georgia, another idiot did the same thing. No clever tactics, no commando-like stalking or use of cover. He just walked from victim to victim and shot them where they hid. Anyone with a gun could have stopped him cold after the first shots were fired. Anyone. He turned his back to his next victim while he took his gay old time yakking about how cruel the world had been to him. SHOOT HIM! Slam him! Do something other than cower.

In Fort Worth, Texas, yet another evil goofball followed the same pattern. Shoot, stroll, yak, stare, yak, point, shoot. What an absolute sitting duck he was for someone with a gun and a spine. Hell, someone was able to point a video camera at him. Why not a .45?

Typically, these mass shooters know they will not be

resisted in a nation of cry-babies. Buford Furrow alledgedly avoided three Jewish institutions because they had some semblance of security on the premises. Buford shouldn't have been on the streets anyway. But California's so-called justice system released him early from prison after he'd been convicted on charges of assault. So then Buford alledgedly prowled around looking for a Jewish center with no security so that he could shoot at people with total confidence that he would meet zero resistance. Bad guys are classic cowards. But the horror of it all is it appears nearly everybody subscribes to the cowardly lion routine. Even Eric Harris and Dylan Klebold in Littleton, Colorado, were nearly robotic in their methodical slaughter. After emptying a double-barreled sawed off shotgun, one calmly knelt with his back to

> How dare politicians continue to pass insane laws forcing good, law-abiding people to be defenseless and helpless.

grown adults and athletes, sniveling, while he conversed with his next victim for minutes on end. He fired twice from an obviously two barreled shotgun, folks! Somebody take it away from him and beat him senseless, PLEASE!!

How dare the media of this land fail to bring up these points. How dare politicians continue to pass insane laws forcing good, law-abiding people to be

defenseless and helpless. As concealed weapons regulations were close to being upgraded in numerous states,
progress was abandoned by denial-infested bureaucrats
who followed violent events such as the school shootings and bombings with what? Punishment for bad
guys? No, that would be too obvious. Instead, they call
for more legal restrictions on the *law-abiding* majority.
What role in God's good name did concealed weapons
permits play in these tragedies? Not one of the shooters
had a permit. Not one! I'm just a guitar player, but I
assure you, had I been around when any of these violent
events unfolded, I would have refused to stand idly by
like some wimp. The Long Island commuter shooter
and the brutal cowards who have terrorized schools,
cafeterias, offices, churches, and day care centers—all
could be, and in some cases have been, stopped by
courageous responsible citizens. Give back to a law-
abiding man the right to a concealed weapon, and he
can stop a felonious madman from perpetrating a
tragedy. Simple, commonsense tactics would dictate to
take reasonable cover, while positioning oneself for a
clear shot with a clear background. Next.

Of course there is always running, crying, whimpering, and hiding. Over my dead body. Unlikely.

Call 911 and have 'em bring a dustpan and a
broom. All they can accomplish is clean up after the fact.

Whether they clean up good guys or bad guys is up to "we the people" who still give a damn. Are we men or are we mice? The answer to that should scare anyone with a soul and a conscience. But not if they have a spine and a gun. ✗

[CHAPTER 6]

THE GREAT TEXAS
MACHINE GUN MASSACRE

LET'S GET ONE THING straight: I've hinted long enough—I love guns. The more, the better. The more shooting, the better. The more ammo, the better. So logic would cause one to surmise that ol' Hunka Ted would just go crazy for machine guns. It's so true. Oh, the very pronouncement of the word sends shivers up my backbone, and my right index finger begins to vibrate uncontrollably. With much pride, I proclaim I'm an extremist! How else could I author "Wang Dang Sweet Poontang" for God's sake?

With the intensity of my career, I have brought all sorts of wild folk out of the proverbial woodwork.

The rapid sequential pulsations of an M16 held tight in my hands, virtually spitting out a torrent of lead, is truly ballistic heaven. My idea of a rainbow is an arch

of flowing brass over my shoulder, piling up at my feet
'til the barrel glows a sunrise orange and someone forces
me to stop. Full auto is music to my ears and a sensual
serenade to every bone, muscle, and nerve in my body.
After all, though guns provide an endless list of prag-
matic qualities, none of those quite
compare to the sheer entertainment
fun that a day of good old blasting
away creates. And any blasting is
grand as long as responsible safety
rules are followed. Whenever the
opportunity to shoot machine guns
comes up, I'm there.

**The uninhibitedness
of my music is in
no way associated
with the thought-
fulness and control
when firearms are
present.**

I've never owned a machine
gun, dammit. I have been offered many and admittedly
drooled furiously over each and every one of them. But
because of certain laws, rules, and regulations, I have
never gone through the bureaucratic gauntlet necessary
to obtain the Class 3 license. Fortunately, I have friends
who have gone through that demanding process plus
many law enforcement professionals who have been gra-
cious and generous enough to let me use up massive
quantities of ammo playing The Lead Hose God. And
good golly Miss Molly, is it ever a panic.

On a family vacation cruise Up North just a few
years ago, Shemane and I had seven-year-old son Rocco

and his friend Thompson along when we decided to join Richard Davis at his annual Second Chance Body Armor Machine Gun Shoot. We experienced what can best be described as a legal orgy of firepower that day. Even the seven-year-old boys fired full auto Thompson Tommy Guns, a belt-fed, tripod-mounted Browning .50, an Uzi, and an assortment of legally owned machine guns. They thoroughly enjoyed themselves. Video games have never been quite the same since.

There were hundreds of families at the well-organized event, and a good percentage of those in attendance were law enforcement and military. Rich Davis is the man who has saved hundreds of cops' lives through his invention of comfortable, practical Kevlar body armor, which is worn by law enforcement around the world. It was hard to leave, even after shooting tens of thousands of rounds from every imaginable machine gun. I shot the Thompson .45, Uzi 9mm and .380, M16 .223, AK47 7.62x39mm, FNFAL .308, Browning .50, Sten 9mm, MP5 9mm, an old Burpgun .45, the amazing Glock 18 9mm, S&W 9mm, M60 .308, Mac 10 and 11 in .45 and 9mm, and some exotic stuff I have no idea the origins of. But every yank of every trigger brought a burst of excitement that outshot the burst of lead and eternal rainbows of spent brass. It really could be considered to be one of the most enjoyable activities a family could ever partake in. We all went away that day with big, wide, toothy grins of happiness.

I have also enjoyed full auto fun with the Michigan State Police armorers at their training facility in Lansing, Michigan. There, we fired an M16, an MP5, and a wonderful old Browning .50 that was pure excitement. It is rather easy to learn to control the big noisy lead hosers. After getting acquainted with the initial shock of such rapid fire capability, one settles down and takes simple control. A firm grip and positive body stance is all it takes to control any machine gun for surprising accuracy. A specific cadence is determined right off the bat based on the recoil, rate of fire, action type of each caliber, and action of the various guns. The Glock full auto Model 18 handgun may very well be the most thrilling of all in that it is a pistol with an ultra smooth flow and surprising controlability. With a modicum of practice, the entire 32-round magazine of 9mm ammo can be slammed into a fist-sized hole on the seven-yard line in a spellbinding 1.4 seconds. That's as close to a vintage Gibson Byrdland plugged into a wall of amplifiers as a civilian is gonna get. I have to go through an intense regimen of detox following a few bursts of that glory. If they made 100-round clips, I might not make it.

Now comes the gun numbnut award of all time. Whether anyone can grasp the dynamic that is the weirdness and volatility of celebrity or stardom is up for contention. But know that it is indeed a force to be reckoned with. It can be a source of simple respect, interest, appreciation, confusion, disdain, outright gaga worship, or complete boredom, but all these reactions are thick enough to be cut with a knife. And so it goes that with the intensity of my career, I have brought all sorts of wild folk out of the proverbial woodwork. One such occasion stands out for the sheer insanity of it all.

I was auditioning musicians in Dallas, Texas, back around 1981 or thereabouts, when good friend and hunting buddy Tony Dukes, God rest his BloodBrother soul, brought in a fellow rockdog to show me some of his songs and singing ability. "Sho' 'nuff," I said. "Let 'er rock, boys." We were running through some soulful jams of R&B and rock 'n' roll classics when this young Texan singer decided to show me his tribute to the American fighting men and women of the military. The painful memory of the embarrassment over the Iran hostage fiasco was still on everyone's mind, and this lad had penned a tune to the refrain of "Barbara Ann" by the Beach Boys, changing the title and lyrics to, "Bomb Bomb Bomb, Bomb Bomb Iran." Cute, I thought. But it turned out that once again a rockfan had grossly misinterpreted my love of guns, confused that the MotorCity Madman conducts himself intensely in everything he does; but that the uninhibitedness of my music was in no way associated with the thoughtfulness and control when firearms are present. Thinking that the best way to gain a position with ol' Nuge was surely to do the most outrageous thing possible, he commenced to sing the "Bomb Iran" words with passion and fire, intensely delivering the message of what America should have done in this terrible hostage crisis. We got through the first verse, jamming away wildly and with everyone smiling at the unique twist of lyrics from this old classic song, when our boy reached behind an amplifier and whipped out a Mach 10 .45 caliber machine pistol, and, in a flash, began firing wildly out into the empty steel shed we were playing in. I immediately knew these were live rounds because I could see the glow of the streetlights outside coming in through the now perforated shed walls with every burst of fire and flying brass. Fearing the worst, I lashed out with my right hand and grabbed his gun arm to ensure he couldn't turn toward the band and I screamed for him to stop. With looks of terror on everyone's faces, I yanked the Mach out of his hands and yelled incredulously what in the hell he thought he was doing! We were on the edge of downtown Dallas, with the major expressway winding not seventy-five yards from the front of the building, with nighttime traffic cruising nonstop up and down the city street right outside our parking lot. And 40 rounds of 230 grain lead projectiles just went zinging randomly every which way. Even at the relatively slow velocity of 900 feet per second, these bullets were traveling plenty fast and straight enough to kill well into the inhabited zones all around us. I was dumbfounded and pissed off.

I ripped the damn piece of junk Mach out of his hands, rendered it empty, then read the sonofabitch the riot act, cased up my guitar, and went out to the limo they had rented for me to get the hell out of there. It was no surprise to me that the limo had three .45 caliber holes in it and the driver was visibly shaken. Of course, the idiot did not get the job. He just stood there with a vacant look on his face saying, "Wha' man? Wha's wrong?" Wha' indeedy. Under no conditions have I ever tolerated any unsafe, irresponsible, or any such type of borderline gunplay. In his feeble attempt to impress me, this moron could have killed someone. Who knows where all those .45 rounds ended up. It was frightening, unnerving, and absolutely intolerable behavior.

It is important to note, however, that of the more than 2.5 million Class 3 licensed machine gun owners in America since 1937 when it became mandatory felony law, only two separate incidents of illegal foul play have been prosecuted. And amazingly enough, both violators were sworn police officers who apparently snapped.

One goofball decided on a quick and efficient full auto divorce, and the other corrupt cop filled his drug supplier full of holes. Although the American media makes repeated claims that AK47s are used in crime every other day, the actual statistics from the BATF reports from 1994 through 1999 prove these claims to be totally false. In fact, a review of all crime gun traces for those years show ZERO fully automatic weapons, except for the converted SKS and AR15s used by the convicted felons at the notorious North Hollywood Bank robbery shoot-out. And those clowns were caught by the law just a short time before this event unfolded, but were let go despite the fact that they were caught red-handed with multiple felony firearm violations. Hey, I got it, let's pass some more gun laws. Banning machine guns oughtta do it. Again. 🏹

CHAPTER 7

GUNSPEAK

TRAFFIC IN THE BIG CITY mall was light and easy going. Shoppers strolled here and there with armfuls of bags and packages. Kids darted hither and yon, in and out of the video arcade and toy store. Mothers pushed baby buggies laden with stuff they didn't need. The lunch crowd came and went all around me in the

To be against law-abiding citizens carrying concealed handguns is literally encouraging and assisting evil to have the upper hand.

small cafeteria. I leisurely sipped foamy double mocha cappuccino and awaited the return of my spouse, fearful she may have purchased unnecessary debris. Maybe?! I hate shopping. I hate malls. I hate waiting. But I grinned through it all, relaxed, just glad to be anywhere with the family that I love. Life is grand after all.

My back was to the corner in the little cafe, a position for optimum observation I have trained myself to adhere to all my life. Partly because I enjoy watching people, partly because I want to see someone who may recognize me, as they often approach. But mostly because I like to have the upper hand in the recidivistic hell of a modern world where inept, even corrupt judges have plummeted into the indecent abyss of civil cruelty determining that murderers and rapists and child molesters somehow qualify to shop alongside the good law-abiding citizens of America. Statistics prove that there is not a downtown square block in the free world that does not have a felon running loose. Some black-robed clown with his misguided, socially toxic, Russian-roulette gavel, somewhere, somehow, has paroled, plea bargained, or just plain abandoned common sense to set free an army of demons into our communities. This is a sad, pathetic fact of life we are all forced to live with. Insulting as it is, it is a reality and it is imperative that we acknowledge and prepare for it. I'm just a guitar player, but I have a date with my children, and no brain-dead justice klusterpunk is going to deprive me of that self-evident truth and my God-given right to defend myself.

A young woman walked straight for my corner and took a seat at the table next to me. She smiled and lit a cigarette. She said hello and looked the other way. I smiled and returned her salutation politely, then immediately noticed two men across the aisleway walking determinedly towards us. I registered a stern if not angry look on both of their faces when they came close to the woman. One sat down next to her while the other tough guy stood with both hands on the table, bent over in her face, and began shouting. The venom was flowing, and it was clear that we had us a full-fledged lovers' quarrel from hell here. The female defiantly squashed her butt out and stood abruptly to leave. The seated man grabbed her violently by the arm and threw her back down into the seat with a loud bang; an ever-intensifying screaming session continued to build steam. The dangerzone grew fangs. Idiot time was upon us.

I was now in serious code red alert—Condition Red—and passersby were straining and twisting their necks to get a look at the escalating commotion. It was then that the larger of the two men turned abruptly toward me, leaned straight into my face, and yelled as loud as he could asking just who in the hell I thought I might be! Before I could respond, he threatened me bodily harm, alleging a sinful relationship between the female stranger, my mother, and myself. At this point, the two men viciously yanked the woman out of the restaurant by her hair, dragging her on the floor, causing a major ruckus.

The mall crowd seemed to vanish from the vicinity of the melee, and the men began kicking and punching the woman savagely. My male instincts compelled me to intercede on behalf of the obvious female underdog. My mind was made up that if not neutralized, the actions of these two perpetrators were well on the way to becoming life-threatening. I rushed to the eye of the storm and pulled the larger perp from his grasp on her arm, spinning him around and yelling at him to leave her alone. His response was a worst-case scenario as he swung a hard right hook toward my head. He had fifty plus pounds on me, and fear ran through my veins.

I instinctively ducked and backed off hoping for de-escalation. But horror of horrors, the larger thug shoved his right hand into his jacket and instantly whipped out a large hunting knife as he fell to his knees beside the now struggling victim. My mindset confirmed a life-and-death situation and was now surging on auto pilot. My right hand plunged into my coat, naturally grasping the small Pachmyr grips of my silver Smith & Wesson .38 caliber snubnosed revolver, yelling as loud as I could possibly yell, "Stop! Drop the weapon NOW!" Though it all appeared to flow in a tunnel-like slow motion, I watched the knife swing high over the bad guy's head. My last word—"NOW!"—echoed against the hard mall walls. Just as the hunting blade hit its upper arc, my two-inch barreled handgun came up to center body mass of the savage killer, and as the front sight touched his armpit, the little gun barked twice.

The knife spun to the floor like the monkey's club in the movie *2001: A Space Odyssey*, and the big guy slouched over sideways. My vision was now nailed on perpetrator number two, and he was instantly on his feet lunging for me, screaming with multiple expletives deleted, in blood curdling shouts: "You shot my friend! You shot my friend!" I backed away and screamed back at him to "STOP" as I leveled the gun on his center. I didn't look at his face, but rather, his hands, both of which pulled at his

> We good citizens of the United States have a God-given right to defend our loved ones and ourselves.

shirt producing cold blue steel from his belt. It all happened in a nanosecond. Now my gun was pointing square into his chest, and I fired twice again. He slumped to the floor like a sack of potatoes, sprawling out before me, moaning loudly, his Model 28, .357 magnum clanging and spinning at our feet.

I kicked his revolver and the knife away from their reach. It was then that I saw movement from the first bad guy lying on his belly ten feet away, as he now pulled a gun from his belt. I had a solid two-hand hold on my handgun and aligned the front sight with the rear sight to send my last 125-grain +P round into his neck, just at the base of his head. He collapsed in a heap.

I knew it wasn't over yet and yelled repeatedly for someone to call 911. I was a pure adrenaline wreck but had the wherewithal to keep an eye on the two downed perps *and* the female victim. At this point I trusted no one! Gathering my thoughts the best I could, I realized that my 5-shot revolver was now empty and scrambled to reload, scared to death of the life-threatening environment I had found myself in. I asked the woman if she was alright but instructed her to stay where she was until the authorities arrived. I pulled out my Special Deputy badge and held it plainly visible in front of me just as a policeman arrived.

The bad guys already carry guns. It is time to level the playing field.

Luckily, this hell-raising experience was only a reenactment of an actual death scene. I was part of a special training exercise of Navy Seals, SWAT, security personnel, and other high-stress law enforcement professionals reliving real-life scenarios where trained specialists had been killed in the past. Our guns were real, but the ammunition was a specialized low-powered squib load with small, paint-filled balls called simunitions. Each participant wore protective gear, but the adrenaline was as real as a heart attack. I achieved a high rating

based upon how I conducted myself in this and other sit-
uations, following not only the law but common sense as
well. And I'm just a guitar player.

With more than thirty states in the nation providing "shall issue" concealed weapons provisions, the
facts are indisputable—see, for instance, the book *More
Guns, Less Crime*—that where good guys have lawful
access to firearms, violent crime goes down. You know
why? Because with any Second Amendment-based gun
rights, the good guys properly have a chance to survive
and, if necessary, fight back. Who in God's good name
could be against that? To be against law abiding citizens
carrying concealed handguns is literally encouraging
and assisting evil to have the upper hand. Who would
demand good people remain defenseless? That's cowardly and un-American. The facts speak for themselves.
We good citizens of the United States have a God-given
right to defend our loved ones and ourselves. It is clearly
guaranteed in the U.S. Constitution's Bill of Rights. It is
time to remind our elected officials that fair is fair and
what is right is right. Who could possibly think for a
minute that the Constitution and the Bill of Rights limit
the powers of the government *except* with regard to the
Second Amendment? That's just plain goofy, but goofy
is how some politicians act when they continuously try
to restrict the rights of law-abiding Americans. We

should demand that the law be guided by intellect and the Constitution, not by politicians who would rather punish people who obey the law than people who break the law. It is time to put the pressure of "we the people" on our elected officials and the general media of this country. Follow your heart, your instincts, the Constitution, and the facts. It is time to "keep and bear" without some bureaucrat's stamp of approval. Write, fax, phone, e-mail, and hammer those elected officials that work for you and me. Tell them exactly what it is they are supposed to represent. Send the bad guys a loud and proud notice. Be good, or meet your maker. The bad guys already carry guns. It is time to level the playing field. It is time for good to overpower evil instead of the other way around. 🏹

CHAPTER 8

WANNA GO TO A GUN AND KNIFE SHOW?
I'LL OPEN MY JACKET

I HAVE FIRED, handled, fondled, and carried nearly every handgun configuration there is. For many years, a nice, beefy Smith & Wesson M29 six-and-a-half inch .44 magnum filled the small of my back ever so reassuringly. Sometimes loaded with .44 special rounds, but mostly full-house magnum fodder. Loose cartridges filled my pockets and sometimes a speed loader in each jean pocket. Living on a beautiful piece of wild Michigan farmground gave me many opportunities to hone my marksmanship and tactics. Wild feral dogs and cats were at epidemic numbers in 1970, and they were very cagey, having learned to elude the regional farmers and

I feel wonderfully capable of protecting my family and myself under nearly all conditions. Reginald Denny I will never be.

sporters who knew instinctively that these numbers had to be reduced for health reasons and simple economic sense. Rabies and distemper are a sure thing when populations get out of hand. Livestock and wildlife depredation levels were unacceptable in the hard-pressed agricultural community. Children at rural and suburban bus stops had actually been attacked and injured by packs of stray dogs. The only responsible thing to do was shoot strays on sight. It was the right thing to do then, and still is today.

The first rule of a gunfight, of course, is to have a gun.

In fact it was all this shooting that gave me supreme confidence in my shooting ability. I went through a 1911 .45 auto, .38 special snub, .357 snub, 9mm Beretta, .380 Walther PPK stainless, Taurus 9mm, and a long list of other calibers and styles. Always with ample backup ammo in fast, strong, hollow point design. And I always made it a priority to shoot the hell out of whatever gun I carried so as to intimately know its feel like an old good friend. Holsters of all kinds were experimented with, but I made sure it held the gun secure and well hidden, but tactically accessible.

For more than ten years now, my self defense and hunting handgun rig remains the same. I fell in love with the Glock Model 20 in 10mm. The most accurate and hard hitting ammo available is Peter Pi's Cor-Bon 135 grain jacketed hollow point XTP bullet, screaming along at about 1,450 feet per second. That approaches the ballistic coefficiency of a strong .41 magnum load, but with sixteen shots in your hand right now. Carried in a beautifully designed Galco strongside hip holster and a double spare magazine pouch on the opposite hip, I feel wonderfully capable of protecting my family and myself under nearly all conditions. Reginald Denny I will never be.

I have upgraded the simple pocketknife by the addition of the irreplaceable Leather Man belt tool. Buck, Gerber, and many other quality knife manufacturers produce fantastic plier-knife multi tools that I thoroughly enjoy and depend on. Like my handgun and spare ammo, I certainly consider a belt tool essential to my daily life. Seems I'm always bailing out the lower rungs of the pecking order when they whimper in need of a simple tool. My pleasure.

A gentleman once told me how superfluous carrying a handgun is, as he had lived for seventy-one years and had never had an occasion in which he could have used a weapon for protection or for any other reason. In order to expose his selfish foolishness, I mentioned how we should probably call the American Cancer Society to put an end to all that wasted cancer research, because after all, *he* never had cancer. He had no response. I didn't have to inform him that personally owned and carried firearms have saved millions upon millions of innocent people and continue to do so today. How dare anyone deny anyone else the most basic of God-given rights to defend oneself? If indeed we have the "right to life," that right can only be experienced if we can keep ourselves from being killed. Just a thought.

But much more important than caliber, ammo, color, action, or design of our chosen handgun package, the most important factor is *mindset* followed closely by *tactical awareness*. Deadly force is deadly serious stuff. Not everybody is up to it. In fact, people like Bill Maher on his ABC *Politically Incorrect* TV show and his talented guest comedienne Elayne Boosler actually admitted to me on one of my many appearances on that show that if faced with an assailant, they would not nor could not use force to defend themselves. By no means with a gun. Damn shame they don't believe their lives are worth saving. Damn shame they would force a law upon everyone else, thereby denying all of us who do believe our lives are worth saving from being able to do so. For the life of me, I cannot comprehend the dismissal of life's value by these sorts. Tragic. Laws guaranteeing the defenselessness of good people are unnatural. Over my dead body. Or better yet, theirs.

There are a gazillion gun stories in the naked city,

and all of them are worth contemplating. First it must be grasped that literally *trillions* of rounds are fired legally, safely, and responsibly for every shot fired criminally or in a dangerous, illegal manner. A review of sales by the ammunition manufacturers, especially in recent years, proves this beyond a shadow of a doubt. And of course we will hear none of this whatsoever on the six o'clock news, that's for damn sure.

> As goes the projectile, so goes the soul.

It is equally compelling to note that the vast majority of successful acts of self-defense with a firearm—some estimates by reliable sources put them at over 2.5 million annually—are by individuals, ordinary citizens with no training whatsoever. Somehow in this modern world, natural, powerful, and good instincts cling on tenaciously. The first rule of a gunfight, of course, is to have a gun. There are no bad guns.

Those souls who believe their lives are worth protecting and saving should get a gun right away and keep it real handy. Any gun will serve you well as long as you put forth adequate effort to become confident and proficient with your choice. My recommended approach would include basic instruction from a knowledgeable person and substantial range time. Familiarity with both the function of the gun and the tactics of getting it into action could well save your life. And at the very least, the discipline will go a long way in quality of life upgrade in all other endeavors. As goes the projectile, so goes the soul. ✗

CHAPTER 9

BLOODBROTHERS

THE VIOLENT STORM had left the entire city's northside crippled. In an ever-growing dynamo, Ma Nature had spoken in hellraising, flaming tongues. Power was lost three days previously, and fear ran wild. Refrigerator and freezer contents were rotting by the hour, and potable

Land of the free and home of the brave or town without pity where dependency is the way of life. Choose one and shut up.

water was scarce. Older citizens' medicine was running out, and a state of panic metastasized over the cityscape. Destroyed, crumpled heaps of ex-buildings were rubble, entire rows of homes were obliterated, a twisted metalscape of automobile remnants appeared as MotorCity gutpile artwork, and nearly every tree in sight was cracked and splintered. Random instances and run-away rumors of crime and looting were vulgarizing everything, and people were getting good and pissed off. Sheer sustenance was job one. As far as the eye could see, an ugly destructozone laid the city to waste. Survival of the fittest was no longer merely a catchphrase. It was reality—tooth, fang, and claw.

One near casualty was averted by a courageous soul when a gargantuan oak crashed into a home, pinning a young toddler beneath its ancient gnarly mass. With the hammering rain still slamming down and a dangerous wind snorting furiously, a man in a camouflage jumpsuit dodged fire-breathing powerlines and jerked a snarling chain saw to life, freeing the terrorized child and his family. BloodBrothers. Survival of the fittest was common law and common sense once again.

Neighbors were helping neighbors, and the goodwill of man ran as wild as the storm. Even before cries of help could begin, good people were scrambling to provide assistance. Backlit by full auto lightning streaks in a black sky gone mad, brave men in heavy duck-hunting garb came a-runnin' with flashlights, tools, blankets, rope, tarps, first aid, water, food, clothing, fortitude, ingenuity, and unlimited heart and soul. Those independent families with wood-burning stoves gathered the cold and weary into shelter and safety. Stored bottled water was distributed and rationed to the needy. Four wheel drive pickups earned their number one sales ranking like never before. There was sufficient survival gear available provided by the more hardy citizenry that had intelligently stockpiled it for just such occasions. It was a traumatic, even deathly week of loss and agony, but the neighborhood was up and running. Peace, calm, and order were restored and life moved on. BloodBrothers.

Lives were saved by future-thinking and history-reading folk who took a lot of teasing, even outright condemnation, by the elitists in the media and some snooters in academia. So-called "survivalists" had been viciously lumped together with "right wing extremists," "Nazis," and general "hate groups" by the liberal press and others. Each side considered the other the "lunatic fringe." To stockpile weapons and supplies was surely the sign of paranoid Klansmen. And conversely, to be unprepared was considered grossly unrealistic, simply inept, and downright irresponsible by the independents. It would have been a long, long wait with one hell of a price tag to rely on government relief in the days following Ma Nature's deathkiss. Land of the free and home of the brave or town without pity where dependency is the way of life. Choose one and shut up.

Now, in the face of an historically not-so-rare disaster, it was the survival loonies to the rescue. For the most part, those best prepared were people who enjoyed camping, rustic outdoor activities, basic preparedness, and simple, rugged individualism. These were hunters, fishermen, trappers, and outdoorsmen who not only knew the fulfilling sensation of taking care of oneself and his clan but actually got a kick out of it. The "kick" was indeed a surge from the not-so-distant ancestral past still alive and well throughout the land. The "shoppers" of the disaster area welcomed these life-saving supplies now, and a sense of reality blanketed the recovering community. Being prepared was not out of date after all. Godbless the last Boy Scouts. BloodBrothers.

Though modern man has mostly come to depend on technical services and indulgent conveniences, the pulse of the warrior rages on—even downtown. Mother Nature can be a bitch, but we love her madly anyway. That flash of history from caveman to European to pioneer to city dude reveals a powerful force of intellect, courage, reason, and creativity that is alive and well. Leaping into the millennium on the backs of strong, uppity entrepreneurs and timeless Jeremiah Johnsons, the pecking order is accurate and in place. And there's not a damn thing you can do about it. Conform to this truism or perish. You get what you deserve.

I am proud that I am one of the last Boy Scouts. When the ice storm hit, my family had food, water, electricity, fuel, heat, and shelter. Who in their right mind would allow a situation to occur that would render his family helpless? If survivalists are looney, then the non-survivalists are just plain wimps. And you know who is the real danger in such a situation? Certainly not those who are prepared and can function on their own, but rather the fools who are helpless and now must seek supplies somewhere since the corner store is leveled or inaccessible. It is the dependents out there who will become the aggressors, for only those who have taken the cushiness of America for granted will find themselves scrambling for food, water, heat, and shelter. And you know what? They are on their own. I am.

It is not being paranoid—but indeed, responsible—to be prepared for an emergency situation: Have a few dozen gallon jugs of water; ample but comprehensive first aid supplies; an alternative heat source such as a wood burner with lots of cut, seasoned wood, and up-to-date, professional-quality fire extinguishers. Store at least one hundred days worth of meals for your tribe, and have a realistic way to prepare them. Have at least a small generator for minimum electric needs with appropriate quantities of fuel. Store items such as flashlights, spare bulbs, batteries, tools, duct tape, toilet paper, toothpaste, soap, diapers, staples like salt, pepper, flour, sugar, cooking oil, powdered milk, dried fruit, pet food, and good comprehensive records of your personal bank accounts, deeds, insurance policies, birth certificates, etc.

All responsible home owners, of course, have ample firepower. A thorough knowledge of your firearms, matching ammo, and self-defense tactics are paramount to family survival. Safe yet readily accessible weaponry is of major importance. Remember, the only block still standing in South Central Los Angeles following the Rodney King debacle were those buildings owned and protected by the Korean shop owners who positioned themselves on rooftops with semi-automatic firepower and had the will to use it. Can you imagine the depth of irresponsible dependency that allows anyone to intentionally render their family defenseless? That's just downright lame. Stand. Survive. Live. Prosper.

And discuss the details of home protection, fire prevention, first aid basics, and designated chores with all family members. These are the kinds of things we have always done at our home. Who's afraid of a slightly extended camping trip? As my song "Tooth, Fang & Claw" says:

I ain't got time for make believing. My time is
short but I'm here to stay. No politics will cure
the grieving. I'll choose my life and I'll choose it

my way. Just like the wolf I'm getting hungry.
The law of the land it is my will. I ain't got time
for staying angry. But I got the time to make a
kill. Watch me kill. I'm gonna live tooth, fang
and claw. I live my life and I live it my way.
Watch me live tooth, fang and claw. And watch
me live an extra day.

To be prepared simply means to see beyond urban
denial. Think about it. In spite of the crazed, blind rat
race for hip decadence, an apparent Kevlar link has been
not only boldly hanging on, but also
throbbing tenaciously like a jugular- **If survivalists are**
clinging hyena canine. Man's worst **looney, then the**
crime against nature has not been the **nonsurvivalists are**
rape-of-the-hills-toxic-bulldozer- **just plain wimps.**
golf-course-mad-land-rush environ-
mental middle finger, but rather simple-minded
disassociation. The more insular our concrete-buffered
lives, the easier it is to deny our own cause and effect.
With every flush of the toilet, every turn of the faucet,
every crank of an engine, every slab of pavement comes
a corresponding global consumptive gulp. With every
head of lettuce, every cotton skibbie, every turn of a
thermostat dial, you will find a corresponding gutpile.
Think about it. One field of cotton necessitates a run-

away multi-bottom plow and disc feeding frenzy, clearly to destroy any vegetation and habitat there may have been. As we pay for this cotton production, that complicit tractor action will kill, dismember, decapitate, mutilate, and destroy every living creature in its path. As in DEAD. Every songbird, gopher, ground squirrel, vole, shrew, chipmunk, worm, bug, snake, grasshopper, horny toad, lizard, Chip and Dale, Alvin, Simon, and Theodore—come hell or high-water—will get whacked and stacked. If any survive the blade of the heavy metal beast worry not, for we shall return when the sun comes up with better living through chemistry and poison their lame, pathetic, legless carcasses with herbicides and pesticides from ag-hell. Terminal Roundup. No bag limit. Kill 'em all. BloodyBrothers.

Like the Great Spirit of our Native American ancestors, powerful self-evident truths pulsate in our guts, and millions of highly intellectual, buoyantly aware individuals have maintained a connection with Mother Earth in their hunting, trapping, and even sport fishing lifestyles. Fishermen were the first to bitch about troutless waters and demanded to know why. Elk hunters stopped the clearcutting of elk habitat. It was hunters who monitored the reduction of bald eagle numbers and fought for their return through undeniably successful habitat restoration programs that we created, managed, and financed. There is nothing like tangible value to inspire safeguarding a commodity. Our air, soil, and water quality is directly linked to wildlife encounter opportunities. Good ground produces. Those of us who cherish these experiences take our stewardship responsibilities deeply to heart. It is a fiery passion. In our face is where we like it.

In Michigan, for example, you can have your truck, guns, dogs, and camper trailer confiscated, be fined a thousand dollars, and go to jail for shooting one goddamn seagull. Meanwhile, mindless bureaucrats will insanely spend a zillion tax dollars to hire the local sheriff and his drinking buddies (a.k.a. professional marksmen) to kill every pesky winged rat they can hit. One year, a million seagull eggs were destroyed with steamrollers for God knows how much apiece. The wise use of renewable resources? Says who! Antihunters are the Crips and the Bloods of wildlife. To hell with them. 🏹

CHAPTER 10

WE THE PEOPLE OR WE THE SHEEPLE?

"I, TED NUGENT, do solemnly swear to support the Constitution of the United States and the Constitution "Baaaaa" or "FREEDOM!"

of this State, and I will faithfully discharge the duties of the office of Special Deputy Sheriff of this State according to the best of my ability, so help me God."

As Eddie Murphy said in the movie *Beverly Hills Cop*, "There's a new sheriff in town. I'm your worst nightmare, I'm a nigger with a badge." His words, not mine, dammit.

And with that, for the third time since 1980, I was duly sworn in as an official Reserve Sheriff Deputy for Lake County in my homestate of Michigan. Then dedicated warrior Sheriff Bob Hiltz and I, with a contingent of other deputies, joined teachers, administrators, and members of the radio, television, and print media and descended upon the Baldwin High School gymnasium where I conducted another one of my DARE programs. Needless to say, it was a glorious day of soul jamming with the youth of America. I had the whole place howling in laughter, then silent and thinking, then singing and communicating, and, ultimately, shoving the middle finger into the face of wimpass peer pressure, with gonzo attitude. The message of independence, individuality, self-sufficiency, and intelligent defiance resonated like a thunderbolt—and it will stick, skullbound. The kids, the parents, the cops, the media, and the professionals all "got it" and celebrated it. The spirit soared high. The stakes are high and so am I, it's in the air toni-i-ight! It's a free-for-all!

"Baaaaa" or "FREEDOM!"

I cannot for the life of me understand the mindset that allows American citizens in this awesome experiment in SELF government to just go about a repetitious, day in day out existence like so many sheep. That, to my thinking, is virtual insanity. The bad rut. Then you die. In reality, a practical death comes much sooner than a biological death, for to merely exist is in fact not to live at all.

The big question is, "Just who is in charge here?" In

charge of our clock? In charge of our calendar? In charge of our paycheck? In charge of our lives? In charge of our kids? In charge of America? In charge of our souls?

When the average American worker (not to be confused with the pimps, whores, and welfare brats) works his and her ass off 'til May 3 just to pay Uncle Sam's bloodsucking taxes, I guess we can accurately identify who is in charge of our time and our money. Annual automobile registration tax sucks. The death tax sucks. The marriage tax sucks. The IRS sucks. Property taxes suck. Personal property tax sucks. Income tax sucks. Withholding any of our earnings is dead wrong. Social Security ain't social and it ain't secure. "Social" and "secure" means individuals and neighbors looking after each other, not some government con job. But too many people—sheeplike—baa complacently, accepting whatever crap government or advertising tries to feed us.

When people still fall for the manipulative, marketing wizards of tobacco advertising to actually pay out hard-earned money to buy an admitted, intentionally poisonous product that WILL kill you, I guess we can accurately admit who is in charge of our decision-making. You do know, don't you, that the facts have been irrefutably proven that tobacco companies scientifically developed, engineered, and added addictive, carcinogen ingredients to cigarettes to hook people? The tobacco companies themselves refer to their products as "nicotine delivery systems." That tell ya anything, cosmo? Oh, and by the way, smoking will not make you sexy, a party animal, cool, or a cowboy, no matter how much you do it. You knew that didn't you? Good. And they don't taste good either. Try licking an ashtray. And instead of slamming me for not minding my own business, I, as your American BloodBrother, merely ask you to think about it. Quality of life upgrade so all of us live as long as possible, as healthy as possible, to fight as strongly as possible. Too much to ask? Don't think so. I make these points because I DEEPLY CARE. I do not take the term BloodBrother lightly. I take it gigantically to heart. I want all Americans to be better, to be willing and better prepared to fight for what we believe in. Equality is for sheep. Be better or get sheered.

And how about the beer advertisements? As a spokesman for Mothers Against Drunk Driving (MADD), I continue my militant crusade to end the curse of drunken buffoonery that runs amok in our country. Puking does not a party make. Wrapping your truck around a tree and destroying innocent lives ain't hip. A beer as a thirst-quenching beverage? Fine. But beyond that, it's all clearly weak people buying into a pathetic image-marketing campaign that getting drunk will get you laid. Sad. I applaud Budweiser and Anheuser-Busch for their generous conservation and prohunting campaigns. Same for Coors and their consistent support of hunting and the Second Amendment. But who is in charge of your drinking habits? Who? Your buddies? Use your brain, comrade. Don't pickle it.

What does all that have to do with my being deputized and a DARE officer? I'll tell you what, it proves I make anti-status quo decisions based on my demand to be in charge of my life. I put forth great effort to lead by example. How dare I!

> I admit, I'm weird. I'm radical. I am a loud and proud extremist. Call me wild, but call me in charge.

For example, I cannot believe that any American citizen does not have a face-to-face, hands-on relationship with law enforcement leaders in his or her community and home regions. I cannot believe that any American citizen could accept having zero input into policymaking by not having a consistent ongoing communication with his or her elected representatives. In the absence of such communication, you in fact have no representation. And that goes to the heart of our eroded Second Amendment rights and diminishing hunting culture in this otherwise great country. Does "we the people" ring any bells?

Today I spoke at length with Senator Phil Hoffman, again. I made my regular call to the good con-

gressman Jim Barcia. Spoke with Senator David Jaye. I
spent the day recently with Michigan State Police
Commander Mike Robinson. I had my regular meeting
with Jackson County Sheriff Hank Zavislak. I met
Monday with Governor John Engler's Hunting, Fishing
and Trapping Heritage Task Force, of which I am a
proud member. Had a private dialogue with Michigan
Department of Natural Resources director K. L. Cool
and Michigan Natural Resources Commission director
Keith Charters. Wrote a letter and placed a call to U.S.
drug czar General McCafferty. I met with youngest son
Rocco's teacher and principal last week. Met with police
chief Steve Sinden. I communicated again with Illinois
state trooper Commander Dan Kent. I wrote a letter to
Illinois Governor George Ryan and Chicago's Mayor
Daley about their ever expanding idiotic nazi gun laws.
I did the DARE program. I rallied with fifty cops and
community leaders on the steps of the Michigan State
Capitol, representing MADD, Students Against
Destructive Decisions/Students Against Drunk Driving
(SADD), National Field Archery Association (NFAA),
National Rifle Association (NRA), Ted Nugent United
Sportsmen of America (TNUSA), Ted Nugent Kamp
For Kids (TNKFK), Brass Roots, and you. Spoke with
Alan Keyes's campaign manager, a New Hampshire
state trooper. Spoke with George W. Bush's representa-

tive and set up a meeting. Called Iowa Republican Speaker of the House Brent Siegrist from deercamp to fight for a dove season there. I spoke with Iowa Bowhunters Board of Director Roger Bowen about ongoing issues. I ran out my cell phone battery discussing important issues here at home with executive director of Michigan United Conservation Clubs Jim Goodheart. Bruce Cull and I had our biweekly conversation about NFAA priorities. I met with the Jackson City managers and the president of the Chamber of Commerce about a new archery range and hopeful future home for the NFAA in America's #1 archery state. TNUSA National Director Chuck Buzzy and I met to discuss the newly formed Whitetail Forever group and the future of Metro Park Wildlife management. Mark Shamblin and I talked about Iowa doves and bowhunting. I took Rocco and his buddies on a swamprun on the snowmobile. I edited four Ted Nugent *Spirit of the Wild* digital tapes last night before bed. I killed another deer. Had a phone call with Bob Miles and Tim Hart at the SHOT Show. Spoke with Dave Ziegler, Bill Norton, and Travis Hall about new Browning products. Coordinated future hunts with Ken Moody. Called Africa. Checked in with Scott Young, Louie Krick, Lenox Bowman, Kevin Kelly, Chester Moore, Charlton Heston, and Ron Thompson. Wrote a letter to *The*

Saturday Evening Post saluting them for the wonderful progun and prohunt pieces. Spent a half hour with four Baltimore, Maryland cops at the Dallas airport this morning strategizing for HR218, the national cop carry concealed weapons bill. Strategized with Brass Roots' Mike Hoban. Called into WJR radio in Detroit to condemn drug punks, antigunners, and antihunters. Proofread *Ted Nugent Adventure Outdoors*. Left a message for Michigan Sportsmen's Congress' Kyle Randal. Called the president of Whitetails Forever. Phoned Glenn Williams, president of Michigan Big Game Hunters Association. Took Shemane to brunch. Took Rocco and his buddy on a bloodtrail then to hockey.

> Ted in the absolute extreme, the whole extreme, and nothing but the extreme, so help me God.

Called Lee Fields in Florida. Working with Texas Parks and Wildlife to extend their deer season through January. Spoke again with *American Archer* television host Tom Nelson about eliminating the minimum age for Michigan's young hunters. Talked at length with TNUSA National Director's Chairman Ward Parker. Took another youngster on his last adventure for Make-A-Wish Foundation. Spoke with Jeff Copeland and Jim Miller at *Ultimate Bowhunter* magazine. Spoke with Van Johnson at *Texas Trophy Hunter* magazine. Tonight I had a great conversation with Dr. Alan Keyes. Every conversation and dialogue dealt with freedoms and rights.

We are not talking a year's, or even a month's worth of activism here, my friends. The list of people I communicated with in the previous paragraph isn't even complete. Many people shake their heads, smile, even laugh at me when they read or hear the likes of the above. I assure you, this is how I live. I AM IN CHARGE OF MY LIFE to the greatest degree possible. Not a day goes by without my taking the simplest of steps to be a "we the people" force to reckon with. I admit, I'm weird. I'm radical. I am a loud and proud extremist. Somewhat like certain Americans who went out of their way to meet the British tyrants at Concord Bridge. Call me wild, but call me in charge.

We will take this country and our freedoms and rights back, one individual at a time. We will take charge of the country when we take charge of ourselves. We will get our paychecks back when we take our rights back. We will get our rights back only when we take them back. Nobody gonna give nobody jack diddly.

Start today. Set a meeting with your state trooper commander, county sheriff, and chief of police. Introduce yourself and your family. Take the kids. Simply let them know who you are, that you are a proud American and eager to help protect your community.

Give them a copy of this book. Sign 'em up as a member of Ted Nugent United Sportsmen of America—and sign up yourself. Get involved. Give them a subscription to *Ted Nugent Adventure Outdoors* magazine. Let them know you appreciate the courage and dedication of law enforcement warriors who sacrifice so much to serve and protect. Let them know how you support and demand law and order, how you appreciate a safe neighborhood. Volunteer your help for various events and programs. Let them know you are there if they could use your assistance when a storm strikes the area, or worse. Get involved with the DARE or PAL programs and kids' events. Do the same thing with your senators, congressmen, and governor. Be on record.

Every sporter should have a personal relationship with his or her fish and game department. Call your local conservation officer and take him or her out to lunch. Call the director of your Department of Natural Resources. Discuss the pros and cons of your region's regs. Ask questions. Offer assistance and observations. Be well groomed, courteous, and confident. These people work for you. Be a caring boss. Speak up and stand up for our American self-evident truth vision.

Ultimately, be a force to reckon with. The alternative is to be no force and to be ignored. If we and what we believe in are ignored, the truth will die. Activism and only activism will put us "in charge." Anything else is slavery. Don't be lulled by the Bill Clintons, Al Gores, and Janet Renos into accepting the unacceptable.

Stay on the True North track. Compared to our apathetic, lame critics, be an extremist. "Live free or die" is extreme. I play extreme, firebreathing rock 'n' roll, greasy rhythm and blues guitar. I eat extremely delicious, awesome meat. I live and hunt with extreme intensity. I extremely value my God-given gifts of senses. The intricate plumbing in a gutpile is extremely fascinating. I love my family extremely. I am extremely dissatisfied with any status quo. Open heart surgery is extreme. Michael Jordan is an extreme athlete. I hate the IRS extremely. I extremely believe in my independence and individuality. I drive an extreme truck. I sleep extremely quietly. I climb trees extremely high. I would shoot a dog in the head that is chewing on a child. I plant an extreme number of trees every year. I use extreme measures to deal with extreme conditions. I would use the most extreme source of water possible to extinguish a fire. I want to be extremely happy. I want to be extremely free. To chose dependency is extremely pathetic. I am extremely proud of my children. Our experiment in self-government here in the United States is extreme. I believe in the Ten Commandments and the Constitution—extremely. If you don't, you are extremely screwed up. Davy Crockett was an extremist. Lewis and Clark were extremists. Rosa Parks was an extremist. Being an extremist in the name of honor is no vice. I am extremely alive. I sleep extremely soundly. Fresh falling snow is extremely beautiful. My ZR1 is extremely fast. Big bucks make me extremely excitable. I am extremely fascinated by sunrises, sunsets, my wife, birdlife, and the Spirit of the Wild. Homosexuality is extremely weird. Jerry Garcia is extremely dead. Pimps, whores, and welfare brats are extremely disgusting. To support laws that force us to be unarmed and defenseless is extremely sheeplike. I am extremely suspicious of Michael Jackson, Jann Wenner, Tom Brokaw, Dan Rather, Peter Jennings, Charles Schumer, Jesse Jackson, Janet Reno, Sarah Brady, the Reverend Al Sharpton (yeah, and if Al's a reverend, I'm the Dalai Lama with a Glock.), Al Gore, Louis Farrakhan, Bill Clinton, Dianne Feinstein, Bill Bradley, the Ku Klux Klan, the NAACP, Jeffery Fieger, and most lawyers and judges. Extremely.

On my 2000 rock 'n' roll roadslam with Kiss, I am the tall extreme guy with the extreme guitar, extreme attitude, extreme songs, extremely loud, extremely sexy, extremely fired up, shooting an extremely flaming arrow, with the extremely talented musicians, extremely passionate. I hope you can join me at one of my extreme Nuge huntcamps for an extreme life experience.

As a brave Marine once stated with extreme enthusiasm: "They're attacking on the left, they're comin' on strong from the right, they are in front of us, they are charging from the rear. Good, now we've got 'em surrounded!" Semper Fi warriors.

Keeping the Spirit of the Wild extremely strong and free, I remain extremely yours, always a BloodBrother, Ted in the absolute extreme, the whole extreme, and nothing but the extreme, so help me God. 🏹

PART II
THE BALLISTICS OF SPIRITUALITY—
YOU CAN'T GRILL IT 'TIL YOU KILL IT

Here's the ultimate recipe. You ready?

Kill stuff.

Add Fire.

Eat.

Burp.

Have a good night.

Thank you very much. Drive safely.

—TED NUGENT

CHAPTER 11

PISTOLERO STEAKAGE

IF GUNS CAUSE CRIME, all of mine are defective. And if handguns are made only for killing people as the actions of Sarah Brady and her lying scum friends like Dianne Feinstein and Charlie Schumer would suggest, then swimming pools are made only for drowning, and ladders are made only for falling off of. Sheer unadulterated nonsense. The percentage of murders committed with handguns is such an infinitesimal number as to be laughable. It is negligent to somehow blame the 99.999 percent of good

Though many may cringe at the thought of whacking cute little furbearers, that kind of uneducated ignorance is the very cause of rampant infestations of disease and even the death of innocent children.

guys for the illegal misuse by the handful of mostly paroled dirt. Remember, the actual numbers from government law enforcement, safety, health, and medical agencies report that larger percentages of injuries and deaths occur from accidents involving ladders and swimming holes than all firearms combined, much less handguns themselves. We won't even look at the carnage from automobiles, electricity, and farm machinery. Bottom line: Handguns and law-abiding handgunners are cool.

Now that we have put the dishonest propaganda to rest let us celebrate the true fact that millions upon millions of law-abiding firearms enthusiasts all across America enjoy a multitude of recreational, Olympic, self-defense, law enforcement, competitive, and sporting use of handguns each and every day of the year. Millions. Every day. And according to the National Safety Council, fewer firearm-related injuries and accidents occur per one hundred thousand usages than those involving boating, skiing, golf, tennis, football, baseball, camping, and a myriad list of activities. The truth is, if you want to be safer get a gun and carry it. Works for me.

I have been using .22 revolvers and semi-autos for small game for more than thirty years. Many a squirrel, rabbit, grouse, and other small game has been brought

to the Nugent dinner table by handgun. Other actions in
.22 magnum, .38 special, .38 super, .380, .45, .40, 9mm,
10mm, .44 special, .41, and .44 magnum have proven
practical and effective for me as well. Some may guess that
the larger, more powerful loads would be too much for
smaller game, but even the .44 mag doesn't destroy much
meat on even a rabbit because the bullet will normally
plow clean through the light critter, disrupting little, and
causing slight tissue damage, but killing quickly and
cleanly. Ya gotta love that. McNuggets should have it so
good.

Living on and managing wonderful Midwest
American farmground most of my life, a readily accessible handgun has made a tremendous difference on the
varmint population in our bailiwick. While rabies and
distemper have reached epidemic proportions across
much of the land, we have no such problem on Swamp
Nuge. Why? Because both of those life-threatening mal-
adies and others like them are a direct result of over-
populations of raccoons, skunks, possums, and an
explosion of free-ranging feral dogs and cats. We have
no such problem in our rural neighborhood, or at least
on our property because we always shoot and kill the
surplus of these otherwise uncontrollable critters,
thereby eliminating the indiscriminate diseased hand of
Ma Nature.

Though many may cringe at the thought of whacking cute little furbearers, that kind of uneducated ignorance is the very cause of rampant infestations of disease and even the death of innocent children. If kids dying of rabies is no concern of yours, you need help and your criticism is unfounded, immoral, counterproductive, and just plain foolish. I haven't the time. Shoot a coon, save a kid. It's that simple.

With a handgun at my side throughout my life, I have taken great pleasure in honing my familiarity and proficiency with my choice of carry gun. While most of my wilderness strolls include a bow and arrows in hand, I gain great satisfaction in casual woodland strolls with only my sidearm accompanying me and my family. In bear, lion, or parolee country, I cannot even imagine being defenseless. That's just plain irresponsible. I see story after deadly story of individuals—even professional animal control officers—responding to actual vicious animal emergencies arrive on the scene UNARMED! Good grief! I'm just a guitar player, but I can't imagine being unarmed. The dog cop that was nearly killed by the pit bull sicked on her in California, quite honestly, deserved what she got. Let me guess, your job is animal control, the call reports a violent, vicious pit bull attacking people, and you show up with a stick and a rope! Sheeeeesh! Next time, baby, bring a damn gun. And when the dog attacks, shoot it between the eyes. Use the stick and rope on the pet owner. Next.

Killing wild rabid dogs in the line of duty is one thing. For sport, I aim for pistolero steakage—for edible small game, like rabbit, to edible big game, like... you name it.

I was walking back up my long marsh-surrounded driveway one cold, winter morning with my five hounds, celebrating allthings Spirit of the Wild. I had just fetched the Sunday paper and tucked it under my left arm when the dogs all flash-pointed a large brushpile. Gonzo, the big chocolate lab, lunged into the tanglement and out the other side erupting a fat, furry cottontail rabbit rocketing away in the snow. In an instant, with the zipper already halfway up on my long, insulated Ducks Unlimited parka, I yanked my Glock M20, 10mm from the form fitting Galco hip holster, and swung one handed on the fleeing bunny. At about 30 yards, just as the scrambling ball of fur was about to enter a beachball-sized hole in the puckerbrush, the handy, Mag-Na-Ported Glock went BANG and the rabbit rolled head over heels into the snow. I never saw my sights, and it could well have been the very best instantaneous shot I have ever made with any weapon in my life. Sure, I'm

> Buy ammo and shoot it up. You will be moved.

bragging, cuz it was sensational, and after all, that's why I shoot all the time, so I can get good. Getting good at stuff is why we live, isn't it? The real point, though, is that if the goofy old guitar player can do it, anybody can, including you. Honing handgun–eye coordination comes from constant—repeat, *constant*—step-by-step rehearsals of the shooting procedure. Shooting is always fun. Shooting always is even more fun. Buy ammo and shoot it up. You will be moved.

My first Alaskan safari came in September of 1977. It represented a hunting kid's dream come true, and I practiced almost daily the entire year before the trip. My carry gun at the time was my beautiful S&W M29, 6 1/2-inch Mag-Na-Ported .44 mag, and I bet I went through at least a thousand rounds of Remington 240-grain soft points that summer. I'd set up life-sized paper deer targets at 50, 100, 150, and 200 yards in my fields and woods, and would go out there with binoculars and bags of ammo. From a sitting position with my forearms resting on my knees, I became deadly at all ranges with that combination. Larry Kelly's Mag-Na-Port Arms expert gunsmiths did a great tuning job, and I knew that trigger like I know my Gibson Byrdland guitar neck. All that shooting developed intense confidence, and it all came together on my third day in the Alaskan wilderness.

George Faerber was my guide. We were deep in the

Alaskan bush, and we had a riot every day. We glassed lots of caribou and black bear and moose from our tent-camp on that magnificent mountainside and had good stalks regularly. Wishing to use my bow on the big game, I wore my big blue Smith & Wesson in a Lawman shoulder rig with a double speed pouch on my belt. Of course like always, I'm sure my pockets were full of loose cartridges as well.

Following twisting, humping ridges and breaks in the tundra, my two-mile stalk came to an abrupt end when I peeked over a hummock at four gorgeous Barren Ground bull caribou still 70 yards out. They saw me, too. They lifted their heads high, flung their enormous antlers back, and trotted down and around the willow-choked ravine. The biggest of the bunch was a real dandy to this flatlander, so I dropped my bow and hustled to the high point before me just as the bulls cleared the line of brush. I sat down in the wet lichens, and, in a ballistician ballet, cold blue pointed straight at the running beasts from solid arms on solid knees. The red front ramp of the Smith's front sight swung slow and smooth on the largest bull's chest, and at about 150 yards, the other bulls opened up and exposed the big boy. The hammer came back, I took a deep breath, and the revolver went BLAMM! A resonate WHOMP came back to me as the bull's head dropped, 240 grains of lead smashing his shoulder bone and penetrating both of his lungs. He crashed face first into the tundra as the other caribou vanished into the wild. I looked back at George through my binoculars and saw him hold a clenched fist skyward, as pleased as I over the instant kill on the good bull. As a handgun hunter himself, we celebrated with the Great Spirit that night with fresh-roasted backstrap filets in the lap of God. 🏹

CHAPTER 12

ROCK 'N' ROLL SPIRIT REHAB

THE SONIC BOMBAST continued to ring wildly, almost painfully, in my ears after yet another year's tour. And I liked it! Two hundred-seventy-seven sold out, ultra-rockin', insane

They got high, and they're all dead. I went hunting, and I'm still Ted!

nights on the road, and I felt like I could go forever. A young man knows no bounds in the adventure of musical exploration, and I craved every delirious minute of this craziness. The fire blazed high and hot.

But in the last few weeks from the windows of the jets, rental cars, limousines, hotels, and tourbus, a dramatic change was taking place all around me. The air was cooling off, the wind had picked up from the northwest, and a hint of color was apparent in the deciduous

timber along the heartland corridor. Increasing numbers of waterfowl were visible, and the hair on the back
of my neck seemed to be at attention. A powerful, deeply
resonate instinct called out, and I found myself more
fidgety than usual. There was something in the air, and
I welcomed it like an old good friend.

Back in the early 1970s I made a promise to myself
that I would never miss an opening day of archery or
gun deer season, or at least a week or two of grouse and
woodcockin'. No matter what. And it drove my business
associates and accountants batty. But it was the intense
anticipation of this spiritual, earthly ritual, as it helped
steer my priorities of family, health, and quality of life
that brought balance to my maniacal rock 'n' roll
lifestyle. The challenge and dynamic calm of the hunt
would shut me up, shut me down, and bring peace and
a strong sense of belonging to a much bigger, meaningful natural order. My mom and dad taught me this
throughout my upbringing with our annual fall treks to
the North Country. These family experiences flow
through my memory bank like cleansing white-water
rapids of reality. Up North had taught me True North.

Throughout my post–high school years, I had
watched peer after peer, sometimes heroes, sometimes
friends, fall over dead like so many sheep to slaughter
because of their failure to prioritize quality control. With

Young Ted—guitarboy.

Young Ted (center) and his gunsmoke cravings.

Ted (center) with his early band out of Chicago, the Amboy Dukes.

Ted and his hero and dad Warren Henry Nugent.

Ted and Shemane
"Life is a series
of bullseyes and
backstraps."

Ted and his hunting
and life mentor,
Fred Bear.

Tribe Nuge
(clockwise from left)
Sasha, Toby, Rocco, Starr,
Shemane, Ted, and Gonzo.

The Tribe in '99.

Ted and his son
Rocco Winchester,
the pigkiller.

Ted and his son Toby
the deerhunter.

Father and son of the Mystical Flight of the Arrow.

Toby and Ted on their annual father-son Michigan duck opener.

Ted, Michigan Governor John Engler, and World Series hero Kirk Gibson, at a Sportsmen for Engler Rally.

A member of Governor Engler's Year of the Family Council,
Ted is surrounded by Rocco, Shemane, Kareem Abdul-Jabbar, and Governor Engler.

Ted demonstrates gun safety at the Queen of the Forest program.

Charlton Heston, Ted Nugent, and G. Gordon Liddy.

Steve Vai and Kenny Wayne Shepherd on the *Ted Nugent Show*.

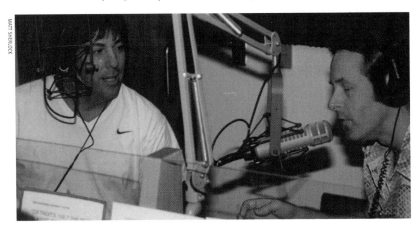

Jeffrey Fieger on the *Ted Nugent Show*.

Ted and Congressman Sonny Bono.

Ted and Shemane with
the Rootin', No-More
Tootin', Shootin' Ballistic
Twins Joe Perry and
Steve Tyler of Aerosmith.

Ted and Shemane with John F. Kennedy Jr. and Carolyn Bessette-Kennedy.

Ted with his signature
Gibson Byrdland guitars
and Conan O'Brien.

Ted and Garth Brooks.

SHEMANE NUGENT

SHEMANE NUGENT

Ted and James Hetfield of Metallica.

Screamin' non-stop for thirty years.

Ted and Sammy Hagar.

"I shoot back."

Ted with an HK automatic.

"No bird is so wonderful as a wild turkey encountered at dawn under a gunmetal spring sky."

Texas triple play.

Venison Hombres—Opening Day
1999, Michigan.

Rocky
Mountain
high.

Magnum
force.

Ted in the hotbed cradle of man.

Cape Buffalo meets Ted Nugent.

Ted handgun hunting in Africa.

Rockin' with the Republicans for MTV.

Adrenaline-
pumping
articulation
of the mind,
body, and
soul.

Damn Yankees
for America.

Gibson Byrdland guitar played by the ten Motown digits of doom.

Ted astride his favorite 2,000 pound buffalo, Chief.

Rosa Parks with a loud guitar.

their failure to focus on a pure, natural, legal, and healthy alternative activity, like my hunting, they lined up for the imbecilic drug and alcohol infestation that was everywhere. Brian Jones, Jimi, Janis, Jim, Michael Bloomfield, Keith Moon, John Bonham, James Jamerson, Greg Arama, Blind Owl, Bon Scott, John Belushi, Jerry Garcia, Kurt Cobain. Zombies on parade. They got high, and they're all dead. I went hunting, and I'm still Ted! Next.

With my hunting activities becoming more enjoyable, more intense, and more visible over the years, the excitement and joy has gotten contagious to those around me. A perfect example of this is my friend Joe Perry of Aerosmith. Considered by millions to be the number one rock 'n' roll band in the world, they had their most successful year ever in 1999. Along with such mega success comes mega pressure. In their position they face offers to make gazillions of dollars that could have them booked 365 days a year. But having come through a harrowing substance abuse period of their own, they have lived their share of hell, and they thank the Good Lord for their good fortune and survival every day. The two biggest stars of the outfit, right out front taking the lion's share of pressure, are lead guitarist Joe Perry and frontman Steven Tyler. You want to know what thrilling recreational pursuit they have discovered to destress and escape? Shooting. And I mean massive, extended, high power, even fully automatic shooting, shooting, and more shooting. The so called "Toxic Twins" have miraculously been upgraded to the "Rootin', No-More Tootin', Shootin' Ballistic Twins," and are damn proud of it. Good clean fun is a beautiful thang.

With an ever-increasing collection of firepower, including concealed weapons permits and a Class 3 license in their "Live Free or Die" homestate of New Hampshire, Steven and Joe have found true love in the marksmanship and self-defense challenge. They enjoy compact (as in small and easily concealable) 9mm hand-guns like the H&K P7, Kaur, Walther PPK in .380, some handy .32's and .25's, plenty of new Titanium S&W snubby .38 specials, fullhouse, scoped .44 magnums, and will soon upgrade to the awesome Glock Model 20 in 10mm. Exacting varminting and sniper performance riflemanship is achieved with a Browning A-bolt in .270. The real fun began with the acquisition of virtual lead hosers like the wonderful H&K MP5 sub-machine gun. Now I'm jealous.

Every time they swing through the Midwest on tour I can expect to get a BBQ alert from Steve or Joe with a request to whip out the venison backstraps and a load of mesquite for the smoker grill. And it's then that I know I must set up the gun range and get out the bowling pins, steel plate targets, and FBI silhouettes for an impromptu shootout. I am Doctor Fun.

Again, recently, during a day off on their sold-out whirlwind tour of the heartland, Joe Perry came out for an afternoon of ballistic celebration as we successfully made up for our failure to be a part of WWII or other official global shootouts. After a few hours of neutralizing various and assorted targets and reducing a hundred bowling pins into so much fine sawdust, we waded through a sea of shining brass for a little lemonade and BBQ while the armament cooled down. I serenaded Joe with my latest recording of his very own composition, "Rag Doll," which I had just completed for a special Aerosmith tribute CD. He squirmed his approval at which point we strolled to the banks of Lake Nuge where we spent a most joyous hour-and-a-half hauling in slabmaster bluegills and sunfish, one after the other, for the frying pan. With the spirit soaring, we grabbed guitars and let the uninhibited positive inspiration of nature's bounty flow as we co-wrote a new love song titled "Catch Slab Fever." It'sa catchy lil' ditty I think you will enjoy next time the 'gills are on their beds scrappin' for a rumble.

> Joe Perry came out for an afternoon of ballistic celebration as we successfully made up for our failure to be a part of WWII or other official global shootouts.

Settling for nothing less than a full fledged day of outdoor epiphany, we grabbed the old Remington 788 boltgun from the safe, loaded some magazines with Winchester 100-grain softpoint boatails, and decided to hit the sacred wildgrounds of Sunrize Acres to try to whack a big ol' nasty Rusky Porkboar. Can you say, "Day off in Ted's world?"

Joe is a natural beyond the pavement, and he smoothly becomes a predator to deal with. His moves become graceful, his level of awareness buoyant. It is a far cry from the intense rocker that drives record-breaking audiences nuts around the world, and his smile bespeaks his enjoyment of it all.

As we entered the wild habitat of Sunrize, we moved stealthily into the wind, taking our time and studying in detail the dense forest and edges with our binoculars. At one point we saw a massive red hog a few hundred yards ahead emerge from a muddy wallow, but he vanished in a flash. A wild turkey cut through the graphic sun-shafted escarpment, and Joe smiled broadly.

With little daylight remaining, we found ourselves bent over hard, ducking through the thick, tangled pinegrove, searching for wild pork in the cool shadows. With another slow, deliberate sweep of my small Leupold binos, I picked up a slight movement across the alfalfa-clover opening under the dark shadows of the autumn olive puckerbrush and signaled Joe to crawl over for a looksee. Quickly but cautiously, in a single, smooth-flowing movement, he shouldered the little, worn rifle just as a huge, black-, grey-, brown-, and silver-streaked tusker stuck his head above the gnarled vegetation. In an instant the .243 BLAMMED and the beast slammed to the ground with a defiant roaring, growling, almost evil, squeal. At around 80 yards, Joe had placed the 3,000-feet-per-second bullet perfectly through the middle of the 260-pound boar's ribs for an instant kill. It was awesome.

Videographer and ace guide Jim Lawson was right there with our "Spirit of the Wild" digital video cam running the whole time. We all raced to the fallen beast where Joe delivered a "coup de grace" with his H&K P7 9mm just for good measure, and high fives were traded all around. We knelt side by side with the dead animal and Joe and I were silent, each reflecting on the dynamic occurrence that comes with every instance of taking an animal's life to feed our own family. Whenever one witnesses the completion of this flawless cycle, especially by one's own hand, we are genuinely moved by the Great Spirit. With the call of a distant crow bringing the moment of silent prayer to an end, Joe and I took a full roll of photos for the family memory album, gutted the beautiful porker, and loaded him up for a trip to Mark Ditzel's Wildlife Artistry taxidermy studios to preserve the majestic beast forever. Then it was on to the cooler where the pure flesh would be processed for primo family tablefare. How organic can ya get?

The sun was fading behind a stunning purple, blue, gold, and pink western horizon as we slowly wheeled the F250 across the last bumpy, rutted woodland trail. A pair of wide-winged turkey vultures cast a Hitchcock shadow over the dusty two track ahead of us, and we drove quietly 'til we hit the pavement before we said a word. Then every detail of the day was relived in excited tones, celebrating the shooting, the freedom to do so, the craftsmanship of the quality arms we enjoyed that day, the beauty of the lake and the tight lines and fighting fish, the breathtaking forests and all her creatures, the wonderful sky and sun and clouds. We remarked at the stimuli of the sounds, the sights, the smells, the feelings. We burped a guttural rave for the delicious wild meat we so enjoyed with family and friends and took a long poke on an ice cold can of Vernors ginger ale to top it all off.

Plans were reviewed to do it again soon, and Joe mentioned that he looked forward to more and more hunting, fishing, shooting, and outdoor activities for his family in the future. He and Aerosmith had a few weeks off soon, before the tour of Japan began, and he said this was a perfect way to relax and prepare for a great time off. We shook hands and said "so long," and I knew the Chicago audience the next night would hear some very special guitar playing by a Spirit of the Wild BloodBrother whose licks would be dripping with the juices of bluegill and backstrap filets and the essence of wild sounds he had absorbed into his heart and soul on this moving, rehabilitating day afield. He might even perform "Catch Slab Fever" for 'em. Maybe "Wang Dang Sweet Porktang." Maybe not. 🏹

CHAPTER 13

BACK TO FANG

THE EAR-SLAMMING discord of a million screeching guitar howls ricocheted from one side of my cranium to the other. And the last concert of the tour was eight days ago! Sonic bombast echoed in the night whether I liked it or not. I closed my eyes tightly and pursed my lips, grimacing, yet snickering inside at the stimulating joy of a long, intense career of unadulterated rock 'n' roll outrage. What a damn riot every one of the sixty-two shows this year had been!

Drawing a deep, lung-filling gulp of swamp air, I slowly relaxed, tilting my head back against the rough bark of the old, gnarly burr oak, and began to hear more

> A good roll in the leafy forest blanket is an orgy for the senses.

clearly the distant, soothing birdsong of my precious wild around me, replacing the barbaric six-string twangathon. The contoured grip of the bow filled my hands now, not unlike the trim neck of my handmade Gibson Byrdland guitar—both familiar, old friends of much different hunts. But unlike the loud guitar, this morning's weapon of choice brought with it a silence and peacefulness extremely opposite of the hell-raising music of my thirty-third year on the rock 'n' roll road. Nothing like shifting gears to keep the spirit alive. And this old hunter's spirit was more than alive. It soared on the wings of an eagle, high above the boondock marshland of my morning hunt arena, taking in every subtle detail of the wild ground I craved, like a sun-dried sponge tossed into a raging white-water rapids.

A hunting license is a ticket to the ultimate health spa that the world has to offer. It will cleanse the soul.

The sensual radar always takes a little fine tuning when leaving the pavement and returning to the wild, and if my smile was any indication, the signals were alive and clear. I could surely smell the change. It is sometimes stated that the Spirit of the Wild is not really something that you can put your finger on, it is not something tangible that you can actually touch. But I disagree. I take the time to scratch and sniff the ground, digging a handful of Mother Earth's aroma and snorting it deep into my lungs. I slice open acorns and beech-nuts, absorbing the pleasant, unique scents they offer. I rub walnuts against my sleeve and pantlegs further blending me into harmony with the pureness of my sur-roundings. A fistful of black peat against the cheeks and forehead not only eliminates the shine of my human skin, but it's a one-two punch of olfactory stimuli, the likes of which Chanel only dreams of. A good roll in the leafy forest blanket is an orgy for the senses.

And then it happens. The calm takes on a tangible quality. You exude it. You reek of it. It is bold and beau-tiful. And the pile driving beat of the modern world surely fades into the distance. Rush hour now becomes a fluid peace, a subtle waterfall of awareness and easi-ness. New tastes and feelings come alive, and you become one with the wind. The soul dances to every birdsong and breeze. There is no Janet Reno. All things become positive as long as we are out there. As an opportunity for a family to get to know each other, there probably is no equal. My tribe gets mushy and closer. And all that damn loud rock 'n' roll is not necessarily gone, but off in the background, building dangerous steam for the next sonic bombastic assault. God knows we all need to escape to Mother Nature today more than ever. Get out there beyond the pavement and claim your own. Those renewable resources that bring us life also convey a powerful spirit-recharging fuel that translates into a more dynamic quality of life. Nature surely heals, and the hunting culture has never lost touch with that reality. A hunting license is a ticket to the ultimate health spa that the world has to offer. It will cleanse the soul. It has never failed me.

[CHAPTER 14]

GONZO RECIPE: CELEBRATE THE FLESH

THE DIRTY, BOOGER-FACED
hippie struggled deep gulps of air in
between dope-infested spasms of
poison-induced coughs and wheezes.
Bloodshot eyes spun from side to side

You want the ulti-
mate health diet?
Go hunting and kill
dinner naturally.

like a lost, confused, wounded baby rabbit. Each word
was garbled as if he were choking on a live, madly spawn-
ing tuna, but I could, nonetheless, decipher his slurred
statement, my having been trained by a thousand pot-
smoking idiots before him in the wonderful world of rock
'n' roll. With bubbled spittle forming a slight, discolored
foam in each corner of his mouth and a cockeyed tilt of
his nasty ass 20W50 racing oil soaked clumps of hair, he
spewed with spastic gestures, "Wow, man, at least you

eat the Bambis you murder." Truly a deeply, well-researched observation from my perfect, average critic who gets his dinner from a can or processed and styrofoamed. It was at this point, I believe, he merely passed out and tipped over in his own stench. Flies buzzed about his head and neck, and I moved on. Wow, man, indeed. Kick out the jams, Gomer. Where's Dr. Jack when ya need him?

At least I eat the Bambis that I murder? Say wha'? This delirious grunting nonsense has been stated to me by many a feeble fantasy fan out there, many times over. As a direct result of foolishly buying into the nonstop propaganda of the majority of irresponsible world media gone terminally concrete, it is easy to understand such fantasy and ignorance from people too lazy, uncaring, and shallow to find out the truth. According to that lying media and their fans gone amok, those big, fat, mean, dirty, drunk, inbred, child molesting, uneducated, slob, redneck Bubbas with machine guns slaughter everything in sight, only then to move on in their inexhaustible quest for bloodlust without ever even bothering to touch their victims, much less respect them through meaningful utility. Balderdash and get them all a bib.

Nothing, I say NOTHING, could be further from the truth. Truth be told, in fifty years of hunting campfires around the world, from rough and tumble tent-camps in the northern wilds of Michigan and Alaska, to primal African villages and plush haciendas of the oil elite in Texas and beyond, I have never in my life witnessed nor heard of anything even remotely like that. No hunter intentionally wastes the life-sustaining products of his kills. It is illegal, certainly unethical, and universally regarded by hunters as intolerable. To fail to utilize, at the very least, the meat from our kills is universally condemned.

The lie that hunting is merely sport or recreation is spawned in the comfort of denial and Disneyesque silliness. Thank God the vast majority who do not actually hunt still support us, and have at least a modicum of understanding that the simple cycle of life and death is sacred and inescapable, that hunters are part of that process, and that hunting and fishing, as life itself, is serious business.

Every precious ounce of flesh, bone, horn, hide, heart, and liver is as sacred as the act of the hunt itself, and actually represents the physics of the spiritual equation of connecting the pursuit and the kill. My Michigan BloodBrothers alone consume nearly thirty million pounds of game meat each and every year, and it is unquestionably the finest, most delicious, and undoubtedly the healthiest sustenance available to mankind anywhere.

Some two million foodborne illnesses beset Americans annually, yet not a single case is associated with wild game meat. The hunt is truly a spiritual workout, with the flesh its ultimate reward. And grand flesh it is. You want the ultimate health diet? Go hunting and kill dinner naturally. Each step of the hunt will teach a deep and abiding reverence for the price paid for each meal, and never again will a forkful be taken lightly or for granted. It's not only the best food anywhere, but it is the very best way there is to connect with the reality of nature and the necessity of the harvest.

Wild game meat has no equal. Venison is the term generally used to describe all wild flesh, be it fowl or herbivore, large or small. Tribe Nuge has not bought domestic flesh since 1969, and the quality of our average meal is nothing short of awe-inspiring. Backstrap fever comes in many forms. We celebrate the delicious, natural, pure, organic, high-protein, no fat, low cholesterol dynamo of elk, deer, moose, caribou, buffalo, antelope, cougar, bear, duck, geese, pheasant, quail, dove, grouse, woodcock, snipe, squirrel, rabbit, woodchuck, beaver, wild hog, and other gifts of renewable sustenance with vigor. It is good to know exactly where one's food comes from. Hands on cause and effect provides valuable lessons in environmental responsibility. You can't deny a gutpile.

There is no trick in preparing game for the table. If

every step of the hunt is taken to heart—from the intense studying and understanding of wildlife, through marksmanship proficiency and woodsmanship skills, right on down to the gutting and butchering of game—that dedication will form a lasting bond that produces a certain respect and value for this life-giving commodity. The cycle works and there is no pretending or avoiding. One of the greatest compliments I've ever received was when an animal rights clown called me a "butcher." And a damn good one thank you. Sharpen them knives.

> Tribe Nuge has not bought domestic flesh since 1969, and the quality of our average meal is nothing short of awe-inspiring.

Clean, cold, and fresh. Those are the three magic ingredients for a perfect meal. Cleaning the carcass properly in the field, keeping it as cool as possible before aging, cooking, or freezing, and finally serving it in a timely manner are the keys to premium quality tablefare. If these steps are followed, heaven will be on your dinner plate and in your gut.

Fieldcare is the first step, and diligent care must be taken to remove all entrails and body fluids efficiently and thoroughly. Plenty of books and videos are available on the market to show blow-by-blow detail, but there is still no better lesson than hands-on by an experienced master. Be sure to taste their game meals before you conclude their mastership. Then proceed slowly, with care, and common sense will steer you properly.

Aging game in a cold environment is always a good idea. Only pork and bear call for limited hanging. Deer and small game will benefit greatly from the aging process and become more tender and tasty with time. Aging a deer for ten or more days will break down the enzymes and bring out the wonderful and unique flavors that excite us all. Even if you can't wait ten days, hold off for a few. Storing and aging at temperatures between 33 and 40 degrees Fahrenheit is best—35 degrees is perfect.

Once the family-sized portions are cut, any recipe will do. From plain hunka venison to venison game pie—any type of game, prepared any way you like it, will bring a different taste sensation to every meal. Here's a simple example: Pick a flesh, any flesh. Cook slowly over hot coals, but elevated away from intense heat. Baste and brush with a goop made from butter, olive oil, brown sugar, seasonings, and preserves of your choice (our favorites are raspberry and apricot).

The real trick with game is to NEVER OVER-COOK! We use Mexican mesquite, oak, cherry, and hickory coals made of half-seasoned wood and half-green to keep the smoke coming. By constantly brushing the yummy slop onto the meat, we can determine when a nice singed crust is formed, while keeping the inside rare and juicy. Wild pork is okay like this, but bear should be slightly more done. But even with bear, don't cook to the core. Oftentimes we add a good mustard and honey to the baste as well. Let your imagination be your guide. If a grill is not available, a roasting pan sizzling with everything, including the baste, cooked at 450 degrees, will work just fine. Just keep basting the meat.

We follow the same procedure with sliced peppers, potatoes, rutabagas, turnips, eggplant, celery, asparagus, earcorn, apples, squash, and onions.

With each stroke of the basting brush and with every turn of each piece of food, exciting flashes of the hunt and ever stimulating animal encounters come flooding forth. Each shift of the wind is remembered. Every wild birdsong echoes. The pulse quickens as you relive the shot. When you responsibly procure your family's dinner by hand, each meal becomes a sacred rite, and the reality of life and death is undeniable. It is good, and so is the feast. 🏹

CHAPTER 15

BIRDHUNT WORKOUT

TAE-BO, STEP AEROBICS, kick boxing, jogging, Hi-Energy workouts. Hell, that's pure wuss world wimpland stuff. And they actually

The worse the weather, the better the birdhunting.

pay to do it! Now, mind you, I'm all for anything that resembles exercise or any good workout in an embarrassing world of 50 percent obesity, especially among children. But treadmills, stairmasters, and rowing machines? Forget it. The best exercise is woodchopping, treeplanting, or just cruising the wild. But if you want the ultimate productive workout, lace up a pair of waterproof hunting boots, grab a shotgun, fill your pockets with shells, call the dogs to heel, then head straight into the nastiest sawgrass marsh wildzone you can find and prepare to magnahump and sweat up a storm. That will separate the sheep from the warriors.

You need to get out when the rain is as close to snow as it can be in October. That's how it was for me, the rain whipping sideways and peppering my face like microscopic birdshot. My hat brim was pulled as low as possible to save my eyes, but I looked up, down, to and fro anyway, scanning every direction for the form of an exploding grouse or woodcock against the small openings to the gunmetal grey sky. It was one of those mystical days where I quit my morning bowhunting treestand early on a hunch. The weather went from great to awesome (bad to worse for a nonhunter) and the building nor'wester brought with it visions of migrating timberdoodles, my favorite game bird in the world. Me and the setters could barely stand it.

With the truck only twenty-five yards behind us, the flutter of wings erupted to my right as the mottled 'cock catapulted for open, dark sky, a red setter nipping at his tailfeathers. Having learned long ago to load the gun immediately and shut the door quietly, I was ready. The short 20-gauge double swung with my eyes and barked instantly as it caught up with the towering featherbomb, ending his ascent abruptly. As the word "fetch" left my lips, a second doodle winged hard and fast behind me and to my left, and I had to shove the safety forward just as it clicked back. Yanking the little gun between popple saplings and tag alders, the barrels swung and covered the second bird just as he cleared the understory and bang-puffed him cleanly. My smile stretched from ear to ear as I broke open the shotgun and stuffed two more lowbase #8's into battery without missing a beat. Both birds were brought to hand simultaneously, and I stuffed the soggy prizes into my game bag and hugged and kissed both dogs wildly. I was so happy, I was drunk on life.

We hiked, climbed, waded, stumbled, trudged, and walked that day, like so many others before and after, for mile after sopping mile, and I never felt tired for a minute. As the wet birds and occasional bonus duck, goose, rabbit, hare, and squirrel filled my vest, the weight and bulk pulled it back down below my fanny and, in combination with my saturated clothes, represented quite the ballast. Deadfalls, beaverponds, and muck-bottomed creeks were negotiated all along the way but were taken in in almost ballet-like stride. Every pocket of brackenfern, popple, and alder-choked cover represented a gold mine of bird-encountering excitement, and I plodded on, unstoppable. The worse the weather, the better the birdhunting. The more impenetrable the terrain, the better the birding. And the dogs! They are unquestionably in hound heaven, working furiously to find a bird for dad. God made hunting dogs to hunt. I know he made this one.

If you have never tried upland gunning, now is the time. A short, well-fitted, open-choked 20-gauge, low-base 7 1/2 shot, 8's or even 9's, preferably a birddog, and, ultimately, a son and/or daughter, and you're on your way to heaven. Any breed dog will do *if* you spend adequate time training it with birds and guns, but setters, labs, and spaniels are the favorites for the job. And my God is it *fun!* The training is *fun*, the shooting is *fun*, and the hunting is absolutely *amazing*. And with unlimited public ground in most states, you can't go wrong. Right now, the grouse population is peaking again after a nearly twenty-five–year slump, and though woodcock are scattered, there are still plenty of birds to chase. And I do mean chase. You *will* put in the miles, and you won't feel a bit of fatigue because it is so exhilarating humping from cover to cover. You are driven by—almost blinded to—the effort.

> I was so happy, I was drunk on life.

You will learn to naturally identify the best bird holes after a while. Young three- to five-year-old aspen growth where it meets patches of ferns bordering low, wet, alder-clumped thickets are nearly guaranteed bird-zone for both grouse and woodcock. I always carry some magnum steel loads for the occasional beaverpond full of mallards, wood ducks, and sometimes Canada geese. My dogs have been encouraged to tree squirrels, too, so a .22 handgun and a few magnum 6's are always handy.

You will, like myself, find yourself trudging up another spectacular, firecolored ridge somewhere far from the truck and the pavement as the day comes to a close, not realizing your legs have carried you far beyond what you thought was their limit had it just been a normal stroll. But with the incredible stimuli of dogs and birds and wind and nature, buoyed by the challenge of wingshooting, you won't even realize you've had a workout. To this day, I am not sure whether the cardio-vascular benefits of the hunt outweigh the spiritual upgrade, but I do know this: I come away a better man following every walk on the wild side, soul to soul with the good Mother Earth and all her season of harvest glory. You will see it in your smile. ✕

CHAPTER 16

TIMBERDOODLE DANDY

TEARS STREAMED DOWN my rosy cheeks as my birddogs gave me a confused and cockeyed stare. I wildly laughed out loud, sobbing, full tilt and alone except for the hounds' goofy looks. My face was bloody and muddy, my left boot remained muck-bound with my heavy wool sock soaked and as black as the peat that claimed it. An orange cap bobbed overhead, snagged by a Hawthorn briar, and my little 20-gauge Browning lay before me in the soup. I'm spread eagle on the edge of the wetlands, hysterical. If a wildman guffaws in the forest, does he make any noise? Let me assure you, he do.

The wildground warrior feels no pain if the habitat smells just right and the mystical acrobatic flight dance of the thunderchicken and timberdoodle is imminent.

The whole exhilarating, nutso Michigan October marshland scenario unfolded innocently enough, but the intensity of this ultra birdhunt represents adventure that legends of the fall are made of. Unless you are an addicted woodcock and grousehunter, I will have to guide you patiently into the netherland of fiery bracken-ferns, shining golden popple leaves swaying in a breath-taking, sun-drenched canopy of yellows, oranges, reds, and greens. Incendiary habitat for the gods of the hunt. We three fearless, intrepid, Natty Bumpo pups plunge madly where no sane creature would dare tread. All in pursuit of a few ounces of magnificent upland fowl that ignites the hearts of hunters everywhere.

The American woodcock is a cute little migratory bird that fascinates us. Rusty and mottled with a 3-inch, worm-probing beak, his pungent scent is the ultimate for arousing a hunting dog's instincts. Sir Timberdoodle Dandy's flight is explosive and erratic, humbling the best of wingshots. His sidekick, the ruffed grouse, is upland royalty with a claymore flush and a bag of clever escape tricks guaranteed to test the very best of well-trained shotgunners. It is the stunning, challenging habitat they share that drives us most of all. Both game birds provide hard-earned and delicious, succulent tablefare fit for kings. And lowly ol' guitar players with a limp.

The wall of tag alders and dogwood appear to

mere mortals to be virtually impenetrable. But I say unto thee, "*au contraire*, el city-kid concrete breath." The wildground warrior feels no pain if the habitat smells just right and the mystical acrobatic flight dance of the thunderchicken and timberdoodle is imminent. Hell hath no flurry like a mad woodcocker deprived.

It was another perfect day. Fifty degrees cool for hard workin' birddogs like us, a magnificent blue sky with scattered puffballs of white, and a slight breeze in our face. The autumn colors were coming on strong now with every invigorating punchy hue decorating the landscape with a firestorm of dazzling, flamethrowing beauty. Toddy, my little Brittany Spaniel, was showing young Blacky, the crossbreed Lab, the demanding ropes of thoroughly covering birdground well within range of my short barreled, chokeless 20-gauge skattergun.

We had walked a ways in easygoing, marginal cover to let our legs stretch a bit, and now we were about to enter the dangerzone. This small twelve-acre chunk of bird heaven was stumbled upon in 1975 while I was following a meandering creek, a young man searching for peace with nature. I found it. And today, as always, the good Mother Earth opens her feisty arms with a snicker. "You can wallow in my gifts, but you will pay, whiteboy!"

I hand-signaled Toddy to cut left into the pucker-brush hellzone, and I clawed my way into the tangled scrub right behind her. It all happened at once in a flurry of hyper moving sequences. At "1001" a grouse erupted to my left, but the little Browning wouldn't swing through the brambles. At "1002" my hat got yanked from my sconce and the gun snagging limbs whipped violently back into my face, stinging

Hell hath no flurry like a mad wood-cocker deprived.

and cutting my neck and cheeks, while at the exact same moment, a fat woodcock spiraled straight up for blue sky, twisting and backwinging beakstrong amidst the maze of young popple regrowth. It was at this point that the black barrel of my shotgun somehow found the rising "doodle" and the light target load of chilled 9's busted the quiet. As the feathered projectile folded and began to tumble down, a second "cock" catapulted from in front of Toddy's nose, ahead and to my right. I fell to my knees and shoved the gun against the tightly woven branches, finding the little booger just as he broke canopy. Round number two barked at the gorgeous clear sky with the small brown bomber centered. Blacky was on the first bird, Toddy on the second, me in a twisted, torso wringer with a vulgar sucking sound pulling my LaCrosse rubber boot right off my left foot, when bird number three fluttered wildly up and straight ahead. Only three rapid seconds into the thicket now, and I was determined to kill this third bird in a row.

So I whipped my bootless foot into the slop in front of me and swung the little automatic thataway all in one flurry touching off my last shell, and miraculously the bird buckled and fell back to earth.

But my forward momentum got the best of my imbalance, and now I was freefalling facedown into the black muck, empty gun smoking, dogs a-runnin', slop a-flyin', Nuge a-floppin'.

It was at this point that the laughter began uncontrollably. I had done it. A limit of woodcock in three seconds flat, just about blinded by Ma Nature's eye-gouging fingers, almost crippled by leg sucking black ooze, and nearly beaten to death by angry saplings. But, dammit, me and the dogs were very, very happy. A bit whacked, bootless, bloody, wet, and muddy, but this is the life.

My wonderful wife, kids, sister, and family are sound asleep around the fireplace in our little northern wilderness log cabin as I write this. Geese are beginning to talk on the lake outside the bedroom window as the sun peeks behind me over the east ridge. The dogs are smiling and snoozing in their kennels. Pure, well-deserved flesh of fowl soaks in the fridge. Nearly fifty years of joyous, moving memories flicker brightly in me like the warming oak logs on the hearth, all for fast, beautiful, small birds, happy dogs, and wildground that turns me on. The red lines of scratches and scrapes on my face actually hurt so good, I'm still laughing.

CHAPTER 17

GOODBYE, POPEYE

ALL TRUE STORIES end in death, a wise man hath said. Uh huh. Seems a Nugent era has been completed as I return from a very special wilderness excursion on our Michigan homeland. Paco the Wonder Dog was a

> Any man that is blessed with one good hunting dog in his life has been truly blessed.

magic hunter. The proud, regal Irish Setter retrieved more dead stuff than any hundred hounds. He was a big part of my growing up. He was very understanding and forgiving of my errors. His son and daughter, Popeye and Pinecone, were officially daughter Sasha's and son Toby's dogs, but they let the old man go afield with them at will. It is said that any man that is blessed with one good hunting dog in his life has been truly blessed.

Lucky, lucky me thrice, for these great red dogs were unbelievable. They'd fetch the neighbor's kid if I gave a nod and a wink! The woodcock! The grouse! The pheasant and quail! The squirrels and rabbits. Woodchucks too! The crows and starlings. Pigeons and blackbirds. Sparrows! Doves! Oh, the doves!

A fresh, tingling snowfall is lightly painting me and the land now, making everything new again. Snow is like that. It is eerily peaceful out here. Heavenly, even. The fat, digging tires on my Honda four-wheeler work doubletime to make way through this wild topography as I tread some sacred turf, cutting stunning, white-draped timber ridges, crossing pure untouched reed beds and marsh, climbing the #1 squirrel rim on earth, and end up in the pretty little creek that bisects our beautiful property. I'm deep into the woods now. Our woods. One–two–three–four–five–six–seven tawny, graceful deer smoke through the heavy stuff ahead, and a fivesome of black ducks rise at the bend. It is here that I pause and carefully cradle the last of the killer bloodline of phenomenal Nugent red setters, for Popeye has joined his dad and sister, teaching why sacred ground is indeed sacred. This turn in the dark water is where we always crossed together, guaranteed to put up a timberdoodle or two every time. Silence and a slight gurgle. So now, like a hero sailor, I lay Popeye to rest in the frigid winter waters of his favorite huntgrounds. He's frozen now, like the earth around us, and I feel good saying *adios*.

I didn't sleep again last night, creative juices gushing through my system, writing lyrics, Teditorials, outlining crusade maneuvers, and basically just keeping my fire screaming. Popeye was sleeping his last. Great way to go. This punchy, no sleep condition I'm in makes me more emotional but not really sad. Like my hunting and life mentor Fred Bear, these dogs got plenty of licks in and the time is natural. A full, grand life, living their ultimate existence for their hunting design. These hunt dogs hunted full time.

The snow is tranquilizing and beautiful. It falls heavier now, and Popeye disappears as he hits his bend. I back away but take the long way home. I need to cover some more of this ground we hunted together for fourteen years, as dusk settles in. Seems some snowflakes have melted in my eyes and I shouldn't let the kids see me like this. Good hunting, my animal friend. Now you have the right to run wild and free. We will cover forever for you with the new dogs: Gonzo and Moose, the Labs; Toddy, a Brittany; and Kippy—a hunting Dalmatian, of all things! Popeye taught him. We'll get that bird. 🏹

CHAPTER 18

TEXAS GOOSE SLAM

"HERE THEY COME, guys! Hit the dirt!" Master guide Bobby Hale instructed the eight of us to grab our ammo bags and shotguns and dive as quickly as possible into the sea of white decoys all around us. I took his word for it that geese were heading our way because I couldn't see or hear a thing in the silent, cold gray dawn on the sweeping prairies of south Texas. So I did what I was told and swan dived headfirst into the muck.

Like Chief Seattle I, too, consider animals my brothers. And like the good warrior chief, I eat 'em for dinner.

And beyond my wildest expectations, sure as hell, they arrived. And they arrived BIG! Very, very BIG! By the time my wounded old rock 'n' roll eyes and ears picked them out of the beautiful dawn sky, the snow geese were right on top of us by the thousands. With the big white birds forming layer upon layer of drifting, falling, winging forms overhead, their honking, squawking, yipping cacophony forced massive adrenaline dumpage, the likes of which I could not have imagined from an avian encounter. With birds landing in amongst us and the seven hundred white decoys, a swoop of about thirty geese formed cupped wings and looked as if they were parachuting right into our faces. I momentarily wished I had an open choked 20-gauge shotgun with #4 shot, but at that instant Steve yelled, "Take 'em boys!" My long Browning 12 came up like a third appendage, the bead covering a bird's head far off to the left, and I joined in with the wonderful symphony of pounding 3- and 3 1/2-inch magnum Bismuth. God, I love the smell of burning gunpowder and relentless small arms fire in the morning!

I believe seven birds plummeted to the open prairie grounds before us as the remaining mass of birds humped a desperate backpedal skyward. It was at this point that the sound of a 50-gallon, empty metal drum being thwacked by a huge 12-pound sledge cut the morning air, as Bobby Hale's big 10-gauge Remington auto pumped a magnum load of BBs into a single bird about 80 yards up and out. It was beautiful as the pretty white goose folded and fell way, way out there near the treeline, 200 yards distant. I took off my hat and held it to my heart, trying to show respect for a dandy long shot. It was the least I could do.

The whole troop of hunters let out war cries of victory with smiles that lit up the entire field. This was without a doubt goose hunting heaven, and we all celebrated intensely the glory of such a magnificent and breathtaking encounter with so many wildfowl. For as our shooter flock increased the distance between us, still more and more geese were heading our way from nearly every direction. It was truly awesome and everybody was scrambling to cram more shells into our plugged guns, grabbing dead geese from tail wagging Labradors, and squirming back into our white parkas and camo for another blast. It was a Nuge party if ever there was one.

And it was like that off and on all morning, right up to about noon, when we figured we had better get outta there so as not to overpressure the nonstop thousands of flying geese that were coming in waves from far off feeding areas. We stacked the bagged birds and counted sixty-seven, with three that we saw drop in a distant field to be retrieved later. Seventy snow geese in one morning. I tried to pick up the stringers of birds, but just half of them weighed more than I could lift! It was fantastic. The dogs lay at our feet with grins of satisfaction, and we all gathered up the cloth decoys with talk and laughter at such a moving experience. Bobby Hale is the Fred Bear of geese, no doubt about it!

With the outrageous overpopulation of snow geese in North America today, desperate measures are being implemented to remedy a serious situation from getting even worse. According to the world's scientists and waterfowl specialists, the breeding grounds in Canada's tundra region can support only about 3 million geese. With the current estimates putting the population at between 6.5 and 9 million birds, it is expected that it will take only one more nesting season to completely destroy an entire ecosystem in that fragile northern area. It is with this clear picture at hand that the game departments, hunting community, and conservationists have decided to get crackin' and reduce the numbers dramatically. The real tragedy is that we have known this was coming for more than twelve years, but certain decision makers actually denied the truth because of politically correct B.S. And once again we are scrambling for damage control because we were not responsible or honest enough to implement quality control. Plugged guns, my ass. It is expected that all regulations concerning the harvest of snows will be lifted. That means no plugged guns, legalizing electronic calls, no possession or bag limits, and, hopefully, access to the Federal

Wildlife Sanctuaries where the majority of geese hang out. If the Feds are wise enough to do all this, I am confident that the hunting community, guided by experts like Bobby Hale, can get the job done. And of course, none of the harvested geese will be allowed to go to waste. I know homeless shelters, soup kitchens, and hungry families across America that would go wild for some delicious, low fat, high protein, zero cholesterol goose breasts on their dinner plate. Hunters for the Hungry to the rescue!

Bobby Hale operates his Third Coast Outfitters out of his home in Bay City, Texas, and is as dedicated a birder as I have ever had the pleasure of sharing the wild with. He and I took turns identifying the geese, curlews, sandpipers, killdeer, crows, song birds, shorebirds, doves, robins, warblers, finches, larks, and other assorted birdlife by their distant song, flight, or movement. I have always been fascinated by our winged brothers and, since a child, sought to know and understand every avian creature I could find. Like James Audubon, I spent much of my youth watching, stalking, and killing samples of most birds so as to examine them intimately by hand.

My BloodBrother and cousin Mark Schmitt and I didn't have fancy drawers filled at the Smithsonian like the pros, but we had grocery bags loaded with every kind of bird we could get. Our killing ended, like the scientists' before us, as we came to better understand the need to save the habitat we share with our fellow animal life. Like Chief Seattle I, too, consider animals my brothers. And like the good warrior, I eat 'em for dinner.

The different lead shot alternatives available make for some specialized marksmanship demands, and I make sure I practice with my chosen load. Steel shoots faster than lead but has a shorter killing range. Bismuth is a lot like lead and my favorite. New alloys like the impressive Matrix loads are gaining new fans all the time. Just be sure you get perfectly familiar with the load of your choice. The goal is fast, clean kills. And lots of 'em. My shoulder looks handsome in varying shades of deep purple.

The good people of Texas have a warm, red carpet hospitality that makes us all feel right at home. The meals are delicious, and the wildlife is spectacular. Some of the guys chased wild boar through the thickets in the afternoon, and a grand time was had by all. We take our hunting time seriously and demand a quality and smooth operation. Bobby Hale delivers in spades on the whole shooting match. My retriever and I are already shaking just thinking about the next goose slam and skies full of ducks and geese.

[CHAPTER 19]

TRES VENISON HOMBRES

MANY PEOPLE HAVE commented to me about how "creative" my descriptions of the wild are in my articles around the country. It ain't me, babe. I'm less creative than I am desperate for enough color and flare to adequately paint in words the spectacle God has blessed us with where I live beyond the pavement. My choice of adjectives and descriptive words are quite lame in comparison to all that I actually witness and absorb in the awe-inspiring outback of the world. Those of us who are driven to participate in as many predator dawns as possible are baptized over and over, again and again, by the hand of God and His stunning, mystical creation. It truly is amazing. Words fail.

Rock 'n' roll is alive and well in the wild.

_____

On this particular December morning, I was tree-bound in the beautiful wilds of mid-Texas, only an hour's drive northwest of the modern metro implosion that is San Antonio. Near the small village of Mountain Home, during our annual Y.O. Ranch safari, I was blessed with yet another heart-soaring hunting experience. The mind races to absorb and comprehend the dazzling bombardment of sensations unique to these mesmerizing hill country sunrises. I mentally gobble them all up like a sensual sponge. It's an orgy and feast for the soul. With intense concentration, I can keep the images with me forever. Each hunt is a hunt for sensual radar shock. Eyes widen and bug out, ears and nose twitch. Goosebumps layer and short hairs rise and quiver. Breathing comes in bursts if you're not careful, and the heartrate hammers away. A spiritual orgasm is neat. And it's legal.

As always, the predawn glow brings squadrons of birds to life, and the scattered singing and chirping from every direction brings a smile to the camouflaged face. Texas has gazillions of bright red cardinals. When they flit about and trade off with the glowing blue-headed, sharkskin-yellow

As the arrow comes back, I slowly repeat, "In the name of the Father, and of the Son, and of the Holy Spirit," then, as my eyes lock on his pump-station entrance rib, the arrow is gone at "Amen!"

green jays, it is an undulating rainbow come to life. Warblers, finches, towhees, and all kinds of avian dynamo burst forth. Bobwhite quail weave in and out of the dark green cedars, light green mesquite, silver black-brush, prickly pear cactus, and red fruited tasajillo, for-ever peeping their morning gathering and feeding calls. All the northern robins are here for the winter, and they divebomb the deep green Live Oak and fiery red and orange Post Oak trees like kamikaze bug fighters. Mourning doves by the hundredfold trade back and forth. Songbirds of every color, shape, and size wing and zing about to perch and feed amongst the thorny thickets of Texas persimmon, coma bush, ephedrine, and the alluring yet poisonous coyotilla red berries all around. The big picture is wonderful, and a close examination through the binoculars impresses me with amazing design and detail. A hen Rio Grande turkey yelps out from somewhere beyond, and you think you see the red, white, and blue of the tom out there in the scrub. This treestand stuff is a riot.

Before you know it, a blazing orange bomb rises slowly in the east and stabs through the scrub, giving every bird an almost iridescent shimmer. Even small puffs of dust created by the dipping and landing birds become multidimensional and show off a certain hew as well, as they rise, fall, and drift in curling waves. The limitless abstract graphic created by the various vegetation challenges the mind and eyes like a giant jigsaw puzzle of the bush. And the wait is seldom long before, somewhere, in amongst the shadows and lines, comes the flicker of a deer ear or tail. Showtime.

There are more than four million whitetail deer in Texas, and I'm out to find 'em all.

The first big game to approach the waterhole this morning would be a trio of handsome bucks, and immediately, they raise the stakes. The fascination with the surroundings goes from intense to hyper. As all prey species do, they circle and zig-zag their entrance with extreme caution, strung tight, ready to leap into the security of the surrounding thicket in an instant. Any wrong move or sound by the predator at this point blows the whole deal. I freeze statuesque, but remind myself to breathe, again. The shakes begin.

The first two prizes are probably two-and-a-half-year-old bucks, nice, but the third is larger, more hesitant, and a much better trophy animal. Six vacuuming nostrils, six radar ears, and six inescapable eyeballs, designed to survive, all created and honed to find the hungry guitar player. With my every move coordinated to coincide with each movement made by any of the trio, I am eventually able to raise my bow into shooting position, hoping for a shot. To double the seemingly impossible challenge, my good friend, Chester Moore, our Ted Nugent United Sportsmen of America Texas director, is sitting just above my right shoulder, manning the digital vidcam, capturing all this action on tape for our *Spirit of the Wild* TV show and video series. Two bodies, twice the scent, and twice the potential noise factor intensify the difficulty of making a bowkill on these high-strung animals. Intensity personified.

With the confidence-building assurance of his two somewhat calmed compadres quenching their thirst, #3 puts his head down to drink, and my #57 bow flexes silently to fulldraw. Predator eyes are locked on his ribcage, and at the completion of my little archery prayer, the 450-grain all-white carbon arrow is in and out of his chest before he can even pivot or lift his head. The arrow skips up from a cloud of dust and sticks hard into a live oak tree as the other beasto hombres beat a hasty retreat into the distant grove of trees and brush, and mine falls out of sight. The birds vanish instantly as well, but begin filtering back within seconds, and all is calm once again in the Texas hill country. Except for my jangled nerves, that is. I'm a wreck. Shaking, I sigh and lean back to compose myself, smiling broadly into the camera. It don't get no better than this.

Then again, maybe it does. Sitting back, waiting to trail the buck, it was only a matter of moments before more deer could be seen a short distance off coming from a different direction. I nock another white arrow, and Chester prepares the camera, as a group of does and small bucks make their way down our trail to the life-giving water. As they close the gap, another dandy buck brings up the rear, and my nerves start their pulsating all over again. Rock 'n' roll is alive and well in the wild.

Just the other side of the oak that holds my first bloody arrow, the eight-pointer stops to test the wind, and I go through my disciplined shot sequence maneuver for the second time in twenty minutes. As the arrow comes back, I slowly repeat, "In the name of the Father, and of the Son, and of the Holy Spirit," then, as my eyes lock on his pumpstation entrance rib, the arrow is gone at "Amen!" KaTHWAK she goes!

Chester got that one on video too, as all hell breaks loose and animals and birds scatter every which way. I follow my buck's deathrun due south with my binoculars and watch as the thick brush consumes him just beneath the orange ball of fire on the southeastern horizon. A smile and thumbs up was all that needed to be said.

It was only eight o'clock, the sun now sneaking in and out from the rolling winter cloud cover. I take a swig from my water bottle and nibble on a Grabber Performance Group high-protein energy bar, feeling mighty, mighty good. I could not have been more certain of the kill shots on these two bucks. The temptation to climb down from our API treestand was strong, but after all, we were in Texas, on the well-managed, deer-rich Y.O. Ranch, and I had more deer tags in my pocket. Heaven is on earth, ladies and gentlemen.

The wind was picking up a bit, and it felt good in the face as the morning temperature rose. After no more than another twenty-minute interval, a tiny flick of white caught my eye about fifty yards out, and once again we found ourselves going into code red alert. A band of whitetails, followed by some axis and fallow deer, were lolligagging their way into our position, slowly but surely. One whitetail doe was an extremely old, sickly looking gal, and with slight hand signals, I motioned to Chester that she was fair game. It seemed as if every time she stopped to nibble, some other, healthier, younger deer would harass her and run her off. At one point, a much larger doe actually slammed her a good one square into her back with a loud, hollow THUD! She scrambled to avoid the bigger doe, and just then, the aggressor chased her right up to our tree, and stopped broadside. THUNK went my third arrow of the morning, blasting through both shoulders of the big doe. She raced for thirty-five yards and was dead in three seconds. What a morning. What an absolutely grand, unreal morning. I actually hung my head and prayed aloud, "Thanks, Lord, for this super-system of renewable resource stewardship stuff. I don't know how You ever came up with this, but it's awesome. You da Man! Amen."

You have to hunt Texas, especially the Y.O. Ranch, to believe it. Some mornings, our hunters see hundreds of head of big game. On this particular bowhunt, I bagged multiple whitetail, sika, axis, and fallow bucks and does. Big fun. Whitetails from the Y.O. are accepted in P&Y and B&C record books and are considered by all to be fairchase hunting. Forty-four thousand wild Texas acres is beyond fairchase. Kids as young as five kill their first deer and other big game animals with us because of the well-managed conditions, superior trained, professional guides, and the varied habitat. I know I'll be there, somewhere in Texas, bow in hand, family and BloodBrothers at my campfire, every winter 'til hell freezes over. Life is too short to mess around. Extreme excitement is my specialty. 🏹

[CHAPTER 20]

THE HOTBED CRADLE OF MAN

WHAT AT FIRST GLANCE appears to be merely a lifeless pile of cold, grey ashes, upon further probe actually contains last night's glowing, red hot campfire embers just waiting to rekindle the body-warming heat of man's best friend: fire. And, too, like the

I felt an overwhelming, powerful presence of much braver hunters than I. I felt a kinship with all around me.

primal scream, desperately howling to erupt in the not so deep of mankind's soul, unless properly unleashed, an incomplete, even deadly cold will prevail. Not me. I'm a hunter.

It was this moving, enjoyable reality that drove me to join the millions of souls across sub-Saharan Africa this morning to squat beside the fire ring, gently uncovering red–orange coals with the shattered end of the God-knows-how-ancient, twisted, dried mopane limb. The earth-rumbling belly growl of a Tuli bull elephant brought depth-charge song to the predawn darkness just behind me across the Botswana border, as the first day's flames licked upward to heat my frozen bones. Cooing doves and chirping songbirds joined the pachyderms and a gentle gurgling from the small waterfall next to me for a dynamic jam session as I stacked hard, gnarled pieces of wood upon the growing fire. I looked to the inner fire through grey and white smoke, my hands rubbing together, and saw there the exact same scene unfolding by the millions and millions with me this morning. I felt an overwhelming, powerful presence of much braver hunters than I. I felt a kinship with all around me. A part of it all. The birds were singing to me. The elephants were starting their day, too, alongside me and my fire. I was but a spear-throwing man on their seamless cave wall. It was great.

How dare hot-tub environmentalists protest hunting, that which is the only hope for this special, unique animal, the elephant?

I slowly hammered these thoughts down onto the laptop screen at fire's edge, then filled my gut with a delicious breakfast of poached eggs, grilled tomatoes, bacon, and homemade toast, washed it all down with fresh coffee with heavy cream and glassfuls of home-grown red grapefruit juice, then grabbed that wonderful bow and arrow for yet another mind-boggling expedition into Africa.

My riverwalk took me along the footsteps of last night's feeding herd of elephants. By the look of smashed grasses, ripped vegetation, and toppled tree limbs, plus the heavy gate yanked from its concrete anchors, I would guess my morning companions numbered twenty or more. I could sense them somewhere around me. Their distinct fingerprinted serving tray–sized tracks told a clear tale of their immemorial survival. Now numbering nine hundred in this Tuli herd alone, more than they have in many years, their severe overpopulation is threatening their very existence—not to mention the apparent destruction of the entire landscape.

Here, where I stalk along the famous Limpopo River, at the confluence of the borders of South Africa, Botswana, and Zimbabwe, the conclusion of the conservation and scientific communities is unanimous that at least six hundred elephants must be killed this year and each year balance must be maintained if there is any hope of saving the fragile riverine habitat. Already, the Chobe bushbuck has vanished as a result of total and devastating annihilation of the entire Chobe rivercourse because of the out-of-control elephant population. How dare hot-tub environmentalists protest hunting, that which is the only hope for this special, unique animal and all biodiversity health that pivots on its resultant balance. Shame.

Flitting whitetailed and ringnecked doves traded with scratching guinea fowl all around me. A shotgunner's dream, for sure. I spent more time stationary than I did moving, doing my best to take it all in. I pushed my mind as hard as I could to feel the pulse of early man here. And I felt it.

I stayed in the shadows, and stepped as carefully as possible, compelled to fit in and not intrude. Where the elephants placed their feet, I too placed mine, and so the soul. There would be no elephants for me today. But I knew that the next day's tracking-safari would bring me face to face with old tusker himself.

I suppose the day started as all days do on safari in Africa. Grand excitement and anticipation for the always thrilling sights, sounds, smells, and feelings. Those bright, licking flames from a glowing campfire ring, conveniently positioned between the chalets and the dining Lappa, greeted us again. With the water already hot, and fresh coffee, tea, and bread to take off the early morning cold, good cheer abounded. Bows and arrows were readied, boots pulled on and tied in the warmth of the fire. Radios were checked, snacks and drinks loaded, and survival packs double checked. Psyche was on primal alert. Tooth, fang, and claw were razor sharp and ready to rock.

I would sit in the reed banks of the Limpopo again this dawn to wait in ambush for the big black–blue wildebeest bulls and the steady stream of impala that usually come to the small waterhole there. But a powerful sensation embodied camp as we departed to a rising sun, for today, the long-awaited elephant kill permit would arrive and the bulls we had seen and heard all week crossing from Botswana to our side of South Africa would be fair game. And I was ready. Good golly Miss Molly, was I ready to rock.

Professional hunter and outfitter Rocco Gioia from Hoedspruit had taken two elephants himself and had guided more than fifteen kills over the years. He and I would work the jungle along the rivercourse with Ken Moody videoing the whole shooting match, and Joe, our expert native tracker, taking the lead. Rocco toted a beautiful Spanish double rifle in .470 caliber and I would use a great custom Remington 700 by Neal Wiggan out of Atlanta, Missouri. Good friend and BloodBrother Dave Matkin had generously loaned me this fantastic piece of riflesmithing built in .375 H&H magnum. With its floated barrel, custom composite stock, stainless action and barrel, an awesome muzzle brake, bolt stop, and 2X6 Leupold scope, this heavy-caliber sniper arm was just what the good Dr. Pachyderm ordered. My sight-in shot with the 300-grain Winchester solids hit deadcenter on the X at 50 yards, and I knew that I and the tool were prepared for this extraordinary task at hand. I was double psyched. My dream of elephant hunting was unfolding right now.

My youth was consumed with hunting reading, and I was always fascinated at the hair-raising stories of hunters stalking enormous elephant bulls in the uncharted wilds of Africa. Now, after all these years of studying diagrams, anatomy charts, and many great elephant hunters' personal experiences, I would put all this information together and pray it guided me to a perfect kill. With elephants it can be a kill or be killed proposition, as it should be.

I had committed to take only a brain shot in order to anchor my bull and drop him on the spot. These marauders were raiding friend Hennie Heyns' citrus groves outside of Messina, and by law the elephants had to be dropped on the South African side before they could trample another fence and head across the Limpopo back into Botswana. The Tuli Reserve had more than nine hundred elephants, and it could support only three hundred. You do the math. Habitat was being destroyed faster than action could be taken. The only right thing to do was reduce the herd for their own benefit and the benefit of the entire Limpopo ecosystem. Scout Nuge reporting for duty.

My Samaria Safaris hunt unfolded like a picture-perfect storybook dream come true. Trailing the beast deep into the jungle of riverine forest vegetation, visibility was at a minimum and the danger factor accelerated exponentially. After a long, arduous, twisting spoor, we came upon a table-sized clearing with steaming fresh elephant dung along the beaten path. Joe stopped abruptly with his hand raised high over his head to signal an immediate halt and silence. He slowly crouched to his knees and pointed dead ahead to a shadowy patch at the base of a tall knoll with a tangle of heavy vines and a gnarly ironwood tree on its sidehill. He looked right into my eyes, and I knew we were in the presence of Sir Tembo. I duckwalked to Joe's side and strained my eyesight into the dusky darkness, and there, 60 yards ahead, was Mr. Tuskerdoo. Now the fun begins.

Getting into position for a specific broadside brainshot on a jungle bound tusker is a bitch to say the least. At this stage of the game, I stayed out front and inched forward slowly, real slowly, as if on eggshell land mines, being as quiet and invisible as possible. The gory

166 God, Guns, & Rock'n'Roll

details of dead, squashed hunters who made mistakes flashed into my mind. Big gulps of dry air came in spurts. I focused and tried to breathe easy.

Conscientious step after deliberate, conscientious step brought me to a dark hole in the thicket, and I eased the stainless .375 barrel into the crotch of a thornbush and breathed through my mouth. Was I supposed to breathe through my nose or my mouth? I forget. No time to think about it, I had to be ready. More ready than ever. He lifted his Mack truck–like head and turned it slightly one way, then the other. I knew what a perfect frontal brainshot and a perfectly broadside brainshot were, but these angles caused me concern. We waited. He shifted. I shifted. Safety off. Safety on. A baboon screamed somewhere way off, I think. All of a sudden the elephant seemed to freeze in place. So did I. There was no world outside the distinct tunnel from my eyes to his head. I was at once frantically alive, yet trancelike. It was cool. Was it getting too dark?

I whispered to Ken that he must be ready and rolling the digital videocam, for as soon as I got a square broadsider I was going to rock. He did, and I did.

With a bellow and flash of fire the .375 roared and the 300-grain solid slammed a point one-third the way from his earhole in a direct line to his eyeball, the center of the tusker's brain. At once he buckled with an instant snap of the head up and back. His legs gave way beneath him and he was on his side in an instant. I ran to him and, though he was totally and conclusively immobilized, drove another round into his heart with mega-penetrating lightning death because that is the law of dangerous gamehunting. And all was silent but for my piledriving heartslammer.

Much celebration went on that night with natives coming out of the woodwork, knives slicing every which way, and much merrymaking at the realization of many months worth of life-giving meat. It all turned into quite a heartwarming display of community teamwork. A tractor was recruited to drag the beast from the jungle and by daybreak it was all divided into family-sized portions. Every ounce of guts, hide, bone, meat, ivory, hair, and spit was claimed for real world, hands-on "wise use," and I was very proud to be a part of it all. I massaged my tattered nerves with delicious South African red wine, good hunting BloodBrothers, and a larger-than-average fire.

It was my first elephant—but I hope not my last. The herds are undeniably beyond the support of their habitat. So surely, I will be ensconced once again, deep within the call of the Limpopo River, with my native friends, seeking that which is good. And it's so damn big, I bet we will find it once again. 🏹

CHAPTER 21

HANDGUN HUNTING IN AFRICA

EACH DAYBREAK STROLL along the Blydes River deep within the South African bush brought my family and me great calm and peace. Birdlife of every description emerged from the riverine habitat bringing beautiful, awakening song to the sub-Saharan scrub. All sunrises and sun-sets are special no matter where you

This night an entire village of natives would dine like kings, compliments of the team of the Great Spirit, Cor-Bon, Glock, and Hunka Ted.

find them, but something powerful glows and grows across the soul and landscape with each incremental warming inch of fiery sunlight, basting the African veldt around you. It's more orange than gold, with just a touch of pink on the rock formations at river's edge. The wind is always gentle at this time, and my step seems more relaxed and slower, yet more alive than usual. It's good for me.

A little later this morning, I would head for the Hoedspruit Airport in south central South Africa for our return home to America after another wonderful African safari with family and friends. The archery cases and all our luggage were locked up and loaded in the combi for the short ride, but I craved one last goodbye walk to watch and hear the behemoth hippos raise white water hell in the pools at the bend downriver from camp.

As usual, for commonsense, self-defense reasons, I wore my Glock M20 in a Galco strongside hip holster loaded with 16 rounds of 135-grain Cor-Bon, bonded jacketed hollow points, with my ever-ready double spare magazine pouch carrying the extra 30 rounds. Hell, you'd think I was going to Detroit.

One's spirit and mind work amazingly efficiently under these inspiring conditions, and it was then that I sensed a tiny movement far off in the thornscrub to my left. Ultra slowly I raised my small Leupold binoculars to identify a large, grey warthog rubbing his fanny against a small tree. I estimated him to be about 100 yards away through sparse grasses and brush, and I filled my hand with the Mag-Na-Ported Glock 10mm in a single, smooth, slow-motion draw. The 250-pound porker paused and looked north as the Trijicon three-dot sight settled on his forward torso, and the slight creep of the 3 1/2-pound Glock trigger came back like it had thousands and thousands of times at the range. I breathed deep, let it out about half way, and the gun went off with a BLAM!

Instantaneously, the WHOMP of the bullet came back to my ears and the beast tipped over in a swirl of dust and kicking feet. I counted 106 paces to the now motionless boar and examined the small hole on his right side and the massive, bloody wound exiting his left shoulder. It was as if I had nailed him with a full house 30-06 deerload. The kinetic energy produced at 1450 feet per second of this superior cartridge is testament to the power and efficiency of good handgun caliber loadings designed specifically for big game hunting and self-defense.

He was stunning in his ugly beastliness with good 6-inch ivory tusks protruding from his nasty prehistoric porcine lips on his wart-riddled face. Warthogs are so ugly, they are beautiful. And the meat is fantastic. This night an entire village of natives would dine like kings, compliments of the team of the Great Spirit, Cor-Bon, Glock, and Hunka Ted.

Ask any adventurer for the details of their most moving moment in the wild, and nine out of ten times it will include a close-range encounter with a wild animal. Morning coffee at the birdfeeder is fun and an important part of my life. Geese overhead always cause me to stop and smile. All animal encounters are essential for my quality of life. But the wilder the setting the better. Sometimes these stories are told by surviving witnesses because many have died at the peak of their excitement. Spiritual orgasms, if you will.

A golden glow against a mountainous backdrop is always defining. A soaring eagle above an endless escarpment of forever timber stirs the soul. But it is the close up and personal dynamic of animal life in our face that will electrify man every time. Like a mega bolt of lightning straight up the kicker, there is something awe-inspiring about the presence of critters within snorting distance. The Great Spirit of the Wild is life-changing when it's off the screen beyond Disney.

Great visionary men like Saxton Pope, Art Young, Fred Bear, Howard Hill, Ben Pearson, Earl Hoyt, Roy Case, Glen St. Charles, Bob Swinehart, Guy Madison, Chuck Saunders, John Mussachia, Bob Munger, Jack Howard, Jim Dougherty, Bruce Gilpin, George Nicholls, Claude Pollington, Ron Chamberlain, and so many others shared their love of nature and archery by promoting the soul-stirring invigoration of the close-range demands of the bow and arrow. There was an undeniable, even unprecedented, excitement to their cries for the mystical flight of the arrow. Their raves about bowhunting were not about taking game, but rather, about GETTING CLOSE in order to take it. Because something BOLD took place on every stalk. Each one of these archers could not get over the thrill of breaking that old 100-yard circle of wildlife's incredible defense network, and they could not get enough of it. The 30-30 would do just fine at 100 yards, but at that range, the bowhunt was just beginning. One would be forced to hone their stealth, stalking, woodsmanship, and natural predator skills to new heights of intensity heretofore unknown in the modern whiteman hunting world. If you think buck fever is something at 200 or 300 yards, try it at 10 and be ready to rock.

> The Great Spirit of the Wild is life-changing when it's off the screen beyond Disney.

So it goes with the growth of blackpowder, old fashioned firearms of all types, and particularly the exploding interest in handgun hunting. It is not, on the average, as exacting as the bow and arrow maneuver, but damn close, and handgunning represents a terrific bridge from long gun to archery. Though many hand-held firearms are absolutely capable of superb accuracy well beyond the 100-yard mark, most pistoleros pursue it for the get-closer challenge. My single shot breaktop

Thompson Contender in .375 JDJ with its 6X Leupold is a genuine 300-yard banger capable of tipping over and cleanly killing anything that walks, way out there. And the related marksmanship demands associated with that are thrills unto themselves. Developing handgun proficiency is far more demanding than long gun work. However, my preference in handgun hunting is open-sighted arms in standard calibers that perform a variety of functions and shooting enjoyments. Like my old reliable S&W M29 .44 magnum and my very favorite, a stock Glock M20, semi-auto carrygun in 10mm.

Having carried a handgun all my life as a practical and essential tool of responsible survival and protection for my family, I believe in having a relationship with this everyday piece of toolage in order to have ultimate, life and death confidence in the weapon and my capabilities with it. To a great degree a hunter's responsibility is close to that self-preservation dynamic, in that, like a life-threatening encounter, a game shot opportunity is nearly always an explosion of instantaneous and spontaneous decision making. It must be a well-trained, second nature response developed through a disciplined system of intense practice and training. There are millions and millions of dedicated handgun hunters out there, and the numbers grow every year. But one must decide to put in the long hours to get good.

It is real simple, and anyone can excel at handgunning if they are willing to put in the effort. I was lucky to have master mentors in my dad, Uncle John, and Mike and Kevin Stellingworth, but there are so many handgun enthusiasts nowadays that good direction, knowledge, and guidance can be gained at most sporting goods shops. What Fred Bear is to bowhunting, Michigander Larry Kelly is to handgun hunting. This legendary man has taken every big game animal on the globe from deer, moose, all the wild sheep species, and brown bear to elephant, rhino, lion, leopard, and everything in between. He founded Mag-Na-Port arms, inventing and perfecting the laser-cut muzzle break recoil reduction system that changed the sport world's attitude toward handguns as a legitimate big game hunting choice. With the help of other handgun hunting technicians like Lee Jurras, Elmer Keith, Hal Swiggett, J. D. Jones at SSK Industries, and others, handgun hunting has been made practical and available to the masses.

And don't think you need a special gun to have a great hunt. Many factory, out-of-the-box revolvers and autos are ready to go. The general agreement in the industry is to stick with well constructed bullets in .40 caliber on up. The .357 magnum, though enjoyed with success by many, is in my opinion marginal on the light side and should be limited to 50-yard and under shots under ideal circumstances, meaning hottest loads on stationery broadside shots on deer-sized critters on down. Nix on the .45 acp. The .44 and .41 magnums are favorites as well as hot 10mm, .45 long Colt, and the specialized single shot handcannons.

Leroy, at The Gun Shop in Quincy, Michigan, took a giant trophy whitetail in south central Michigan last season with a .44 mag revolver and red dot sight. He knows his stuff. Call and talk to guys like Leroy that have experience. Contrary to the lies of the enemies of our Constitution, handguns are NOT made to kill people. Less than .00001 of handguns ever manufactured have been used for illegal activities, and 99 percent of the time were used by sick, violent punks some goofy judge figured oughta be out on the street with us. Be one of the tens of millions of law-abiding handgunners in America, take it to the next level, and go get yourself some organic dinner with a sidearm this season. Practice like mad. Breathe easy and squeeze smoothly, and get out the garlic and butter.

CHAPTER 22

SHOOT, DON'T SHOOT—
THE SPIRIT AS MY GUIDE

BOBBY FONTANA and his dedicated wilderness troop of woodsmaster guides delivered me square into the belly-o'-the-firebreathin'-beast. Screaming wapiti were raising what could only be translated as the extreme rock 'n' roll sonic bombast attitude of the wild. I felt ridiculously right at home. The ponytail was at full mast. My first urge was to join in with the guttural larynx abuse or at least dance like the MotorCity Mad Indian I am, but instead I merely tightened the grip on my bow as I scrambled to loosen my grip on the overwhelming mountain air stimuli.

Who would be idiotic enough to spoil such a natural adrenaline charge with trendy awareness destroyers? Not this projectile-addicted guitar fool, that's for damn sure.

My heavy wool clothes were well saturated now, after a 100-yard GI Joe bellycrawl through rainsoaked puckerbrush from hell. But now I was on my right knee, and from the sound of things, about to meet Godzilla of the Elk Clan, flared nostril to flared nostril. And the punk peers of the electronic rock 'n' roll world couldn't believe I had turned down their poisons forever! You want better living through chemistry, kids? I GIVE YOU HERD BULL ELK TEDSTOSTERONE in mega wads of organic racing fuel injections, IN YOUR FACE! Who would be idiotic enough to spoil such a natural adrenaline charge with trendy awareness destroyers? Not this projectile-addicted guitar fool, that's for damn sure.

So on this emotional flamethrower of a September day in the high country of British Columbia, Canada, I was entering the moment of truth. And as if guided by my (or was it Fred Bear's?) script, the most beautiful, majestic, mud- and urine-encrusted beast showed himself at a short 40 yards, permeating the entire mountainside with his lusty, full rut, king-of-the-hill stench. I sucked in the glorious air all around me and closed my eyes so as not to miss one iota of the soul-stirring standoff. But now what?

God knows I love to kill game with my bow and arrow or by whatever legal means I choose, and the awesome 6X6 was surely within my intensely practiced, high percentage, surekill range, BUT—he was facing me head on! DAMN! My eyes burned a hole deadcenter into the patch of black mud right under his chin as he stretched and screamed.

Strangely, now I heard nothing. Nary a noise. All I could do was concentrate on that 6-inch window to his heart between those arrow-stopping front shoulder bones, just above the sternum, but low enough into a channel that would take my 600-grain shaft deep into his vitals for that sacred kill. Quick and painless. I had done it before on hogs, deer, caribou, moose, buffalo, great big African game, but none of them screaming all over me. His huge ivory-tipped, antlered head heaved up and down with each Rocky Mountain battle cry. Could I time my shot to enter him perfectly as his nose and skull got out of the way? Could I put a Nugent Blade into the grapefruit-sized spot I needed to, at this angle, on this steep incline, all wet, tensed up, and sucking the thin air *very* hard, double humpin' massive spirit?

> One's ethics are determined by what we do when no one is looking. Because He is. True North or nothing.

He turned his head to the side and looked uphill, and my arrow came back hard into the corner of my mouth like it had for millions of mystical flights before.

My eyes lasered into the small pocket but I held the shot. Since he was looking uphill, would he move that way to offer the perfect broadsider we dream of? Or should I let 'er rip right here and now? I held. He looked. I held. Then he stared right at me, I let down my draw and he did a perfectly executed, instantaneous 180 degree pivot and shook his tailfeather in my face. It was over. He was out of sight in seconds, swallowed by the majesty that is elk and God's country. I sighed deeply, smiling a glow of sheer joy for having experienced this essence of the hunt.

Though the possibilities ran through my tortured mind like a stampede of migrating wildebeest, I slumped down into the rocks and vegetation knowing that my decision was, though maybe not the ultimate, a correct one that made me feel as good as I could feel this side of standing over the trophy bull that had provided me such a spiritual surge. I got it all but the meat and horn. And that's a full bag limit for the soul any way you cut it. I can remember the shots I didn't take as graphically as the beasts I've slain. The physics of spirituality go deep.

This is the lesson I share with students at our Ted Nugent Kamp for Kids each summer. The same lesson I instill in my hunter safety and International Bowhunter Education Program (IBEP) students. Even the DARE kids and the classrooms full of young 'uns I teach get the same dynamic lesson of the reasoning predator's special relationship with God's creatures. The meat will come, but the heartbreak of a bad hit and a lost animal is mental trauma difficult to cleanse, for this old hunter and every other one I know, young or old. I guess my dad, uncles, friends, and Fred Bear taught me well. Though I've dangled my share of Coleman lanterns over enough lost bloodtrails in my days, I also know that of the thousands of hunt campfires I've shared with novice and veteran hunters alike we human predators are batting a better percentage than lions, cheetahs, coyotes, eagles, and wolves. Be that as it may, we are the only predators who have to hit the hay each night with our bubbling conscience—it's either surekill or one pissed off, discomforted, sorry hunter.

The simple answer is don't let that arrow or bullet fly unless you are 100 percent confident you are going to penetrate those vital organs necessary for a responsible kill. Take it from a guy who feeds his family exclusively with the game we harvest each year. The right shot *will* come. Wait for it. One's ethics are determined by what we do when no one is looking. Because He is. True North or nothing.

CHAPTER 23

OUTRAGEOUS WITNESSED AND
OTHERWISE LIAR SHOTS I HAVE MADE

I EXPECT SOME inexperienced people and some who think they know it all to have a field day with my

The only good coon is a dead coon.

writings in this book and the various publications I write for. By all means, have at it. But the real joy is that my writings have always been truthful and in the face of my outlando adventure and exciting life's experiences. I understand the need for small minds to criticize and accuse. Some of my advice and claims will be scoffed at. The very premise that I know people have the right and duty to defend themselves will leave those with communist ideologies agasp. So be it. There are even professional ballisticians who will cite certain paper science to dismiss and refute some of my shooting stories herein.

But be that as it may, I stand by them all and further wish to share some of the more outrageous examples of ballistic defiance I have celebrated over the years of firing a gazillion rounds under every imaginable circumstance and condition. Having a gun at the ready for all these years has allowed me to test myself and my equipment to the fullest, and I ain't even warmed up yet. I still shoot extensively and regularly. Just today the hounds raised a ruckus in the tangle down below the house, and I found myself squatting in the soaking wet puckerbrush staring down a snarling raccoon. As Bear, our big wolflike shepherd, whipped the masked marauder against a thornbush, I whipped out the 10mm from an extremely contorted position and was able to doubletap two rounds instantaneously deadcenter into the furred vandal of the wild, killing him. It was only a 3-yard shot, but I did not use my sights, opting instead under the exasperatingly thick vegetated conditions and frenzied close quarter dogfight to simply thrust my gunhand at the target very quickly in between dog lunges. I train myself to do so at the gunrange. One less egg-stealing, rabies-carrying vermin on SwampNuge. The only good coon is a dead coon.

ON A WARM SPRING DAY on the farm in 1971, I was exploring my family huntgrounds looking for shed antlers, asparagus, and morel mushrooms. Racing home on my Yamaha 360 Enduro motorcycle as if I were in the Baja 1000 Motorcross, I was cranking pretty good in and out of the fields and woodlots of our ranch. Though I would never shoot a turkey vulture today, on this day of youthful craziness I saw the huge winged bird sailing high overhead as I came scrambling through a plowed field and decided to see if I could hit him. He was so high up that he appeared to be a speck with wings in the clouds, but like the young dolt I was, I yanked my Smith .44 from my shoulder rig, and with one hand, while still coasting at a pretty good clip, I swung the 6 1/2-inch barrel up over my head and double actioned a 240-grain hollow point his way when the front sight swung past his floating form in a randomly calculated, half-ass lead. Astonishingly, the big bird dropped a wingbeat and began to fall to earth. He was so high up at the shot that his fall took him about half a mile away before he hit the ground, the 44-caliber bullet having hit him in the chest. That was illegal as hell, but to make it worse, I had the bird mounted and used him atop my amplifiers as a stage prop for many years.

WALKING MILES IN THE ROLLING HILLS of Oklahoma on a great day of quail hunting with friend Paul Schlosser and his dad, the discussion went from hunting dogs to guns to women. We had a grand day of

wingshooting and had a good load of birds in the bag.
Paul had mentioned to his father that I carried a pistol
and comments were made about how carrying a gun was
frowned on more and more these days. Not only that,
but without specialized training, it was questionable
whether anyone could become accurate enough with a
sidearm to be meaningfully effective. Paul had seen me
shoot on occasion and began bragging to his father what
a pistolero I was. Now I would never claim to be a great
shot; in fact, I had made it a point to keep my gun-car-
rying tradition a secret and never expose it unless necessary. But Paul insisted I could shoot and I found
myself making the point that with some practice, even
the Beretta 9mm in my belt is capable of some pretty
impressive performance. It had been stated that a handgun is only accurate out to a few yards at best, and I
insisted the gun itself was actually capable of much
more. Paul said, "Hell, Dad, Ted could hit one of those
ducks in that pond way over there!" He pointed to a
small farmpond at least 200 yards distant in which a pair
of mallards were swimming around. His dad laughed
and Paul insisted. After much prodding, I figured what
the hell, slung my 12-gauge onto my shoulder and
unholstered the 92F. Cocking the hammer back, I
looked along the barrel past the front Trijicon night-
sight, and as the entire pond appeared above the

frontsight resting atop the rear aperture, I squeezed one off, and, swear to God, that 124-grain Cor-Bon bullet splashed within inches right next to those ducks as they beat wings up and outta that pond. Paul glowed, I grinned like a madman, and his father just shook his head. I clicked on the safety, holstered the gun, and we walked on.

WITH THE KIDS OFF TO SCHOOL one fall morning, I was preparing to depart for town when my ace mechanic Earl mentioned he had seen a pair of beautiful cock pheasants in the orchard behind the shop. Already feeling a bit guilty for not taking the setters hunting on a perfect morning, I decided at least to let 'em run and get a nose full of hot birdscent. So with streetclothes (clean jeans) and a minute, I cut my wonderful red dogs loose. They knew right away what was goin' on and made a beeline for the tangles of our gamehaven orchard. At first I had no intention of trying to take a pheasant and made no effort to retrieve the shotgun from the back of the truck. But as the hounds made game and got real birdy, I walked in behind them and withdrew my 4-inch stainless S&W 44 from the shoulder holster and made the decision to take a shot if we put the bird up. Earl was watching and smiling from the open door of the shop, wiping his hands on a rag and taking in the beauty that is poetry in motion of intense hunting dog work. At once my oldest dog Paco flash pointed a clump of ground vetch and the gleaming fireball of iridescent plumage erupted skybound twenty-some yards distant. Mirroring his ascent, my short-barreled magnum floated along, and as my steel-filled fist swung past the now rocketing cock, flames spit forth from my handgun, the other white meat crumpling in a shower of feathers to the ground nearly 40 yards out. Earl stopped wiping his hands and our eyes met with a goofy smile of semishock. Only semi because he had witnessed many such unbelievable shots over the years. Flying birds, running rabbits and squirrels, shots that can only be made if (1) you practice your ass off, and (2) you try 'em. And only to be mentioned if there are witnesses.

ANOTHER ONE FOR THE RIPLEY'S Believe It or Not files took place many years ago at the Bow & Bore Hunting Ranch in northern California. Cresting a high ridge with Jeff Roe in his Bronco, we were discussing our favorite handguns. Both of us hopelessly addicted gun nuts, we were giddy and taking our gunlove talk to the extremes when I spotted movement some 600, maybe 700 yards across a vast canyon. (Jeff thinks 800!) Through the binoculars, we viewed a half dozen curly horned rams lounging on the far slope, and I told Jeff I could hit one with my Beretta 9mm. Basically, he expressed much doubt, and said maybe with the 6 1/2-inch barreled .44 magnum I had in a shoulder rig, but no way with the pipsqueak 9. Now mind you, one of my favorite handgun practice routines is longrange shooting in the tradition of legendary Elmer Keith, father of the .44 mag and handgun hunting. Mostly in the springtime, when fields are plowed and hits show up with puffs of dry dirt, a shooter can walk his bullets into the target through trial and error. Having recently completed just such a daylong shootfest, I felt confident that I could do it. Well, strap yourself in. My very first shot hit an isolated ram—my chosen target—square in the hip, the tumbling 124-grain Cor-Bon +P+ round smashing the big femoral artery and causing him to stumble and roll down the steep mountainside. I know it was irresponsible to try such a shot and would certainly never do it again. But I did and it was amazing.

ONE MORE OUTRAGEOUS SHOT for the record would have to include another unbelievable poke witnessed by State Senator H. L. "Bill" Richardson and Sam Peredes, founders of Gunowners of California. We had flown into the rolling wilds of northern California one afternoon to chase hogs, and as I deplaned onto the grassy runway, I asked if I could shoot at a jackrabbit sitting about 100 yards away. At the time I was carrying a Smith & Wesson Model 59 9mm in a hip holster with two spare magazines on my belt. Newly acquainted with these two fine gentlemen, I did not want to give them the wrong idea about my proclivity to crave shooting ops, but in fact I was itching to shoot having been cooped up in the recording studio for a while. Given the OK by my hosts, I double-checked the surrounding area, drew my pistol, took aim, and touched off a single round that flipped the standing jack head over heels. Bill and Sam nodded their approval. Running to retrieve the varmint, I brought it back to examine it and we found the bullet hole in the center of his body. Precision shot placement at 100 yards. It can be done with lots of practice and absolute familiarity with your gun. 🏹

[CHAPTER 24]

PROJECTILE MANAGEMENT MARKSMANSHIP

THE CROSSHAIRS OF the 6X Leupold scope danced wildly all over the buck's body. My lungs were heaving, thumping my chest violently in and out with each strained snort-wheeze. It was not a giant, trophy buck by any stretch of the imagination, but I had run about three miles to circumvent the downwind woodlot in order to cut him off at the marshgrass pass, and I had made my mind up that this backstrapper would be mine! Now to put it all together.

> The ethical hunter kills cleanly.
> That's the rule.
> Accountability is right up there with safety and the law!

I lay in the wet grass, only my head and gun showing over the lip of the field ridge edge. With the 12-gauge shotgun as steady as it could be, my elbows formed a bipod for the long 130-yard shot. He was staring straight at me through the glass as if he could see the microscopic movement of my gun barrel and scope, plain as day. This only exasperated my nerves, and I did not dare take off the safety. No shot yet.

But I remembered what Dad and Uncle John had taught me about trigger control and accuracy as I sucked in a huge breath of cold morning air, snuggled my cheek firmly against the stock, and slowly whooshed it out through my open mouth. The safety tang "snicked" almost inaudibly and about half way through my exhale the duplex reticule slowed then stopped, as if painted on the buck's backbone directly over his shoulder. The Browning 12 roared and bucked as if on its own. I yanked the deergun down out of recoil to see him take the full impact of the 1-ounce slug square through the shoulder blade, faltering back just as I heard the KerWHOOOMP of the lead pumpkinball connect with 170 pounds of dense muscle, bone, and sinew. The buck danced the dance of death in a ragged 30-foot semicircle and fell over sideways with a ceremonial, four-hoofed salute to the heavens. Yeehaaa! Even a blind squirrel finds a nut once in a while.

The green hull still smoked as I pocketed it, and I shoved another live round into my fiveshot magazine for full battery condition one. My walk to the animal counted

131 steps which I have come to calibrate as about a yard each. A longer shot for a shotgun, but easily within certain range for intensely practiced scoped and rifled barreled, sabot-loaded, projectile shotgun marksmanship. From a benchrest, bipod, and sandbags I knew this gun could shoot amazingly tight cloverleafed groups out to 200 yards, IF I could do my part. My part, of course, is disciplining myself to PRACTICE diligently at ALL ranges, and to thoroughly test the various makes and loads of slugs and bullets available for optimum performance. The days of shotgun big game hunting with birdguns ought to be over as far as I'm concerned. It is an exceptionally rare smoothbore that is capable of real field accuracy with solid ammo, and grossly irresponsible to think otherwise. The ethical hunter kills cleanly. That's the rule. And that means endless practice with the right equipment to ensure the job gets done right. Accountability is right up there with safety and the law!

The same basic principle applies to all "projectile management," really. Whether it's arrows from my bow, rocks and marbles out of my wristrocket slingshot, BB's from my Red Ryder, handguns, open sight rifles, or scoped target guns, good marksmanship will only come with certain and intense discipline. And it will all boil down to trigger control, sight picture control, and ignition on target, which will only come with controlled breathing. Breathing is good. Controlled breathing is best.

The good news is that sporters are spending more time than ever afield, enjoying all the shooting sports. We're spending more money, too, with outdoor activities creating a flow of more than $61 *billion* a year into the American economy in related spending. Studies prove that hunting creates more than $3 million *a day*, all year long for conservation programs like habitat rehabilitation (clean air, soil, and water) and wildlife reintroduction. Grand stuff. Mucho dinero, amigos! And mucho fun as a result.

I encourage everybody I know to get out for more casual, recreational shooting with family and friends. Especially *new* shooters. Every year at our Ted Nugent Kamp for Kids, I witness the effervescent glow from children from all walks of life as they cultivate and test their marksmanship skills on the range. They love it! These recruited enthusiasts will make or break conservation efforts and gun rights progress in America, for we all know that the vast majority of conservation and Second Amendment support monies and education comes from the shooting and hunting community. Celebrate hands on!

So get your "hands on" a gun or a bow. Get out to a target range or gravel pit. Set up some targets and let it fly. Always practice ultra safety procedures and wear protection for eyes and ears whenever discharging a firearm, but make the extra effort and discover the thrill of the accuracy challenge.

At my best I'm an OK shot. On average I shoot very average. But I'm getting better since I set out to specifically improve my shooting procedure. I try to make every shot count by getting my mind in "shoot mode," and it has really paid off. That first shot is always the most important shot, and a simple repetitious regimen will make all the difference in the world.

My first smart decision was to shoot more often, thereby getting to know the feel of each weapon intimately. Every arm, every trigger, every bow has a unique touch, and we must know exactly when the moment of ignition/release occurs. Oftentimes, at the range under strict safety supervision, I line up my gun or bow for the shot, then close my eyes just before I fire so the "feel" at the moment of discharge is burned into my memory bank. This must be done over and over and over again so it becomes second nature. The old saying, "Beware the man with one gun" is very true and accurate because it means he *knows* the gun intimately and is therefore ultimately effective with it. That should be our goal. Of course, I want to know all two hundred of my guns intimately.

Shooting is athletic challenge at its finest. Be it gun

or bow, new or old, take a friend or family member, especially a youngster, out shooting at the very next opportunity. My son glows whenever we spend quality shooting time together at the range or in the field. Every kid is fascinated by guns and if we don't train them properly the alternatives are not very pretty. Make it a primary goal to introduce a newcomer to shooting, for as we assist in their baptism by projectile we offer needed guidance, knowledge, and an exercise in self-discipline for young people. Upgrade will come overnight. Learning to excel at shooting sports literally gives kids something to aim for. Life will be a series of bullseyes and backstraps. Who could ask for more? 🏹

PART III
KIDS, FAMILY, AND THE
SPIRIT OF THE WILD

Sometimes you give the world the best you got,

and you get kicked in the teeth.

Give the world the best you got anyway.

CHAPTER 25

THE GUITARKID AND GUNS

FROM ACROSS THE blue-black choppy waters of the Detroit River, a shy sun peaked in and out of the grey fall sky. Gusty winds blew the picnic tablecloth up and around the containers of potato salad, chips, beans, and cold fried chicken as Dad and Uncle John tossed horseshoes into the dirt with an occasional pinging clang.

The rules are simple: ALL GUNS ARE ALWAYS LOADED and NEVER POINT A WEAPON AT ANYTHING YOU'RE NOT WILLING TO DESTROY.

Mom and Aunt Alice sat at the table with their babushkas blowing in the cool autumn wind, constantly talking about whatever women talked about in the *Leave It to Beaver* '50s. Brothers Jeff and Johnny and I chased each other around the trees and shrubs of Detroit's downriver

neighborhood of Monroe, banging plastic and tin cap-
guns at each other in our daily mock cowboy shootout. I
always dove for cover, poking my silver revolver around
the base of my tree, as little of my head showing as possible. Young seven-year-old Nuge had figured out basic
gunfight tactics with no real training whatsoever. I almost
never got killed. Instincts rock.

Our little games of good guy/bad guy were always
fun, but we kept it up only long enough to bide our time
in anticipation of the real McCoy. Family gatherings
with Uncle John and Aunt Alice were excitingly special,
not just because they were wonderful, special, loving
people, but because these outings always included a
little target shooting with various handguns from Dad's
and John's collections. These relaxed, casual plinking
sessions were the highlight of weekend maneuvers, and
I couldn't wait to wrap my little hands around the fascinating pocket guns and touch off my very own, personal,
blazing projectile to see what I could hit.

All of us kids enjoyed it immensely, but I absolutely
loved it.

John had a highly coveted German Luger that I
never learned the origins of, but it shot like a sweetheart.
Dad let us shoot his officer's pocket Savage .32 automatic. And it seemed nobody was really able to hit with
any consistent accuracy, but it sure was a riot blasting

away at tin cans and watching the dirt fly. It drove me crazy when the sessions came to an end, running out of ammo and/or daylight much too early for my shooting desires.

Both gentlemen were stern and uncompromising in their directions on safety and proper gun handling. At no time would we be allowed to point the gun's muzzle in any direction except 180 degrees straight away from everybody. Even the slightest mistake and, at the very least, your shooting was over for the day. A bad move could get you a good cuff in the back of the head and worse. God, I appreciate that discipline to the bone today. The rules are simple: ALL GUNS ARE ALWAYS LOADED and NEVER POINT A WEAPON AT ANYTHING YOU'RE NOT WILLING TO DESTROY. All other safety talk is superfluous. Dad installed a trigger lock on my brain.

My intense cravings for shooting would come close to being the death of me on at least one occasion. On a hot, humid Michigan summer afternoon when I was about twelve, I found myself alone in our Rosedale Park home. After I had delivered my two hundred or so *Shopping News* and *Detroit News* newspapers up and down the quiet northwest Detroit suburban neighborhood streets, I spent the entire morning shooting my bow and arrows and BB guns as usual. But at some point my mind began to wander toward bigger and better and louder shooting fun. It is important to note that Dad was one militant, drill sergeant disciplinarian sonofabitch, God rest his soul, and he planted deep and abiding fear into all of his children. Fear is good and will do just fine in lieu of understanding the rules. Rule violations were rare at the Nugent house, but something that day lured me into trouble anyhow.

I brazenly entered Mom and Dad's bedroom and went right to Dad's top dresser drawer where he occasionally let me borrow one of his neatly folded white handkerchiefs. Many times I had seen the dull, worn gunmetal grey of his .32 in the back of the drawer. I could not believe that I was actually grabbing it and taking it into the basement. I knew for certain that if I were to be caught doing this, the old man would have ripped my head clean off and shit down my neck. He was a drill sergeant in the U.S. Army Calvary at the tender age of nineteen, and he never really let go of the hard-core mindset. He had his original horse training riding crop, a twisted rawhide and metal whip with a nasty ass ball of hard leather at the top, and we children feared it like the hand of God. He never really whacked us with it, but it was one hell of a deterrent.

Nonetheless, here I was, slightly trembling, looking at Dad's gun in my hand, setting up boards in the basement to shoot at. With two two-by-fours upright against each other against the wooden workbench, I took careful aim and tried to pull the trigger. In my state of fear, I forgot to take the safety off, and I actually remember working up a sweat by this time. Fumbling and finally releasing the safety, I aligned the short front sight snug into the notch of the fixed rear aperture, square into the center of the two-by-four and touched one off. The blast was so loud in the confines of the stone-walled laundryroom that it actually hurt my ears and scared the

> This was a gun pointed straight at my nose; literally an open channel to my brain that was cocked, loaded, and, with the safety off, ready to fire.

living hell outta me. It was far louder than anything I had ever experienced when shooting any gun outdoors. The smoke hung in the air around my head and sawdust puffed up and then down onto the concrete floor. I was shaken, to say the least, as the boards tumbled.

And now my fear exploded like another round thinking that neighbors would surely hear the report. I laid the gun on the top of the washing machine and scrambled to clean up the sawdust. I actually took a saw and cut the boards where the bullet entered in a feeble attempt to destroy the evidence. But that was nothing compared to what I was about to do next.

The smell of gunpowder filled the room. I figured I would rub a little Hoppes #9 solvent and a dab of 3-in-1 oil around the end of the barrel to offset the aroma. I was doing all of this without resetting the safety, mind you. Incredibly, I pointed the muzzle of the barrel at my nose to take a whiff in order to smell if I had eliminated the telling stink. This was a gun pointed straight at my nose; literally an open channel to my brain that was cocked, loaded, and, with the safety off, ready to fire. GULP! Not understanding the basic function of hammerless semi-auto firearms—where the recoil and gas discharge from one shot chambers another round, ready to fire—I was committing the cardinal sin of firearm handling. This was not an accident. It was pure, potentially deadly negligence, and there is a huge difference. My guardian angel must have been at my side that day, for I was able to return the Savage to Dad's drawer and nothing ever came of this horrible transgression, though the constant and powerful fear and guilt stayed with me for many, many years.

I use this terrifying experience as a graphic example of what *not* to do when training my own and other children, as well as adults, on the inevitability of the untrained getting their hands on firearms. My parents did good with me, and I have no excuse for my violation. It was certainly not their fault by any stretch of the imagination. Excuse makers be damned. But statistics prove that the percentages are extremely high that a kid is going to encounter a gun. It is going to happen, so prepare intensely.

My first recommendation would be to read the tell-tale signs that kids give off as to their interest level in firearms. At the very least, provide instruction and forthright discipline. Keep all weapons absolutely out of reach of youngsters and encourage them to always *ask* to see or use the gun, and then respond effectively. This way the mystery is minimized. I strongly recommend that most guns be kept secured in a locked, quality gunsafe, but I also highly recommend that a good defense arm be secured yet immediately accessible by adults for its potentially life-saving purpose. With but a modicum of intellectual review of our individual home conditions and layout, a good choice can be made.

My own choice in home defense armament is a 12-gauge semi-auto Binelli Model 90 riot shotgun with open rifle sights, loaded with 2 3/4-inch #4 buckshot in our saferoom, that is immediately grabable but at the same time invisible to the naked eye. Also strategically positioned in our home is an assortment of military semi-autos in hidden locations. All these guns are locked in a safe when we are not at home. I will tell no more than that. But I will tell you, because we have children in our home all the time, these firearms are virtually unattainable by any unauthorized individuals. When kids are at our home we regularly supervise recreational and training shooting sessions. All parents acknowledge their appreciation, and the kids absolutely love it. 🏹

CHAPTER 26

NEGLIGENT DISCHARGES I HAVE KNOWN

OTHER THAN my vintage, all-American, handcrafted, Northern Spruce Gibson Byrdland guitar, fondled sensually by my ten Motown digits of doom, plugged into a bank of outlandishly loud and dynamo hummin' Peavey amplifiers, upon the real-

There is no such thing as an accidental dis- charge, only neg- ligent discharges.

_____

ization that the guy responsible for all those stimulating rhythms and primal screams is actually semi-Caucasian, nothing will get your attention quite like a gun going off when you do not expect it. Particularly if one is trained and experienced in gun-handling and knows the otherwise cel- ebrated ballistic results of such a discharge. It stays with you forever. I share my own painful psyche-ruptures as a result of such experiences in hopes of upgrading our level of awareness and eliminating this rare, but certainly avoidable, mishap. High hopes for sure. And the bottom line remains that there is no such thing as an accidental discharge, only negligent discharges. It is never a hardware problem, always a human mistake. Period. So don't make the mistake.

The vast majority of negligent discharges do not occur where people are paying attention to guns—in hunting camps, in gun owner's homes, or in gun stores. The majority don't even occur in the hotel rooms of rock stars—my good friend Dusty Hill of ZZ Top, who shot himself in the ass with a derringer while pulling off his boots, notwithstanding. Cuz he wasn't. Now that's embarrassing. And though the most dangerous and inexcusable display of shooting idiocy goes to the big city drunken gomers who celebrate all sorts of holidays by touching off illegal-as-hell rounds into the air, the best information available indicates that most negligent, unintentional shots are fired in police stations and law enforcement locker rooms. Understandably, more gun handling takes place here than anywhere else, but remember that this is an environment where all handlers are professionally trained to the fullest degree. So even the best need to be reminded about safety. With all due respect for these great men and women of the shield, let's be careful out there, kids!

According to the National Center for Disease

Control in Atlanta, more kids drown in buckets of water each year than by gun accidents. Buckets of water, mind you. We are not counting swimming pools, rivers, lakes, hoses, and puddles, just BUCKETS! More kids are killed and injured playing sports, skiing, on bikes, skates, skateboards, electrocuted, burned, smothered, cut, bitten, stung, and beaten. These are the facts that the American media, Sarah Brady, and Jann Wenner will ignore at all costs. We must ask ourselves: Why?

Back around 1980, I had recently switched my carry gun from my trusty and ever lovin' sweetheart Smith & Wesson Model 29 .44 magnum to a beautiful Colt Commander 1911 .45 ACP semi-auto. With much practice and experimentation trying all types of ammo and leatherwear, I put together what I was convinced was a dandy rig for daily carry. In a Milt Sparks hi-rise basketweave strongside pancake holster, and three magazines loaded with Speer 200-grain hollow point "ashtray" rounds, I had supreme confidence in the old slabsider carried in condition one, round in the chamber, hammer back, safety on, cocked, locked, and ready to rock, doc. The handgun and I were capable of consistent two-inch groups rapid fire on the seven yard line, and I could keep 'em pretty much centermass in the FBI bad guy target all day out to 40 yards timed fire.

I admit that I had an old-fashioned attitude toward

the Colt .45 and all semi-autos overall. I was fearful of jamming, rendering my defensive sidearm useless. And all the WWII boys I had the privilege to communicate with were unanimous that old slabsides was incapable of meaningful tactical accuracy. Of course, these fears were based on old wive's tales, for with a minimum of sensible care, maintenance, and standard training, a quality auto like the Colt Commander can function flawlessly and reliably even when subjected to rugged field conditions and hardcore street wear and tear. With this in mind, I religiously kept the slide and rails oiled and kept the action dirt and grit free.

With daily practice sessions on the range, my confidence built and I learned to thoroughly enjoy the advantages of the smooth controllable recoil of the punchy caliber and the ease with which multiple accurate hits could be achieved with the incredible trigger action of the Colt. Tactically speaking, there were substantial benefits over the big .44 wheelgun I had gotten used to for so many years. Colonel Jeff Cooper's writings and ravings praising the 1911 were of particular value, and I had turned into one of his biggest supporters.

Upon the completion of one such two hundred or so round afternoon shootfest on my backyard falling steelplate homerange, going through the numerous daily drills I had developed, I holstered up and let my three wonderful Irish setters loose for a run through the orchard before going indoors to begin preparing supper for the Tribe. After a little fetching and wrestling with the hounds, I chained 'em back up and turned to walk up to the house when a pair of blue jays squawked over the driveway into the adjoining grove of apple trees beyond the kennels. Hating the noisy blue thieves of the wild, I spun as they lit onto a high branch about 40 yards off and drew the .45. Though I had blasted many such targets under the same conditions over the years, my aimed doubletaps merely exploded a bunch of leaves and limbs underneath the now departing jays. The dogs raised hell knowing that when Dad's gun goes off surely there must be something hitting the ground for them to fetch and/or chew on. I calmed down the canines and merely turned back towards the house, casually, yet as always, conscientiously swapping the now reduced magazine with a fresh one.

Holding the pistol forward and high with my right hand, pointing skyward in a safe direction, I released the mag with my right thumb while yanking a fresh mag from my left hip belt pouch. Catching the falling mag between my right pinky and the edge of my right gun-hand palm, I slammed home the fresh magazine while inserting the used mag back into the pouch next to the other full mag. With leisurely steps I continued my stroll to the porch as my right hand instinctively found the tight pancake holster opening on my right hip. I was looking at the porch step as the barrel of the .45 entered the leather and my right thumb felt the safety in the up ON position, a second nature move that I had programmed myself into as a last check of the gun's safe condition. Within a few feet of the porch step, I pushed a final shove of the gun into the holster when it happened. I instantly froze, stood statue still with eyes bugged out about a mile or two, trembling. The surprise gunshot translated into a virtual explosion. I didn't even feel the big fat hollowpoint rip through my right hip pocket, shredding my red neckerchief into confetti. The highly destructive self defense round missed my flesh by a blue jean layer and slammed harmlessly into the gravel driveway underfoot. Having my hand on the gun as it went off, I let go immediately, leaving the smoking gun in the holster where the leather caught the slide causing it to remain partially open, unable to complete its cycle.

In a clear case of overreaction, I put the .45 back in the safe that night and went back to a revolver for a long, long time. As I rethink and relive this experience over and over again and again in my mind, to this day I cannot for the life of me figure out what happened to cause the gun to fire. Though I went back to an auto as my prime carry gun a few years later, and have confidently carried my Glock Model 20 for many years with no problems, this mind-numbing occurrence has indeed stayed with me to this day. It increased my level of awareness and respect for just what can happen. One cannot be too careful and must at all costs adhere to the basic gun safety laws as if one's life depends on it. Because one's life does depend on it. In the year 2000, I performed more than 120 concerts. That represents at least 300 acts of unholstering, unloading, disassembling, reassembling, reloading, and reholstering actions, backstage, including the same procedure many times each week before checking and picking up bags at airports and so on, and I did so with nary a mishap. Practice makes perfect as long as one practices perfectly.

Here's another true story about the absolute necessity of triple-checking for safety. I remember it was an hour before shooting light on November 15, the always mesmerizing traditional opening morning of deer season, deep in the wilds of Michigan's Manistee National Forest, and the Great Spirit was on fire. Mom and Dad, Uncle John, brothers Jeff and Johnny, my small children Sasha and Toby sound asleep in their bunks, and our good friends, father and son Mike and Kevin Stellingworth, were all there in our beautiful Big Timber wilderness log home. A fresh skiff of light snow blanketed the rolling forests of God's country out our big picture window overlooking the small lake, and the intoxicating olfactory stimuli of fresh coffee, bacon, sausage, eggs, toast, and roaring oak logs in the fireplace that make up deercamp's pungent hunter's cocktail filled our world. Life was peaking.

This traditional morning was as big a deal as anything in life to a million hardy Michigan deerhunters, but more so to me. Dad, Uncle John, and my brothers certainly enjoyed the hell out of it, but they took it much more casually than I did. For many years, I would seek out the next year's calendar just to circle in red my precious November 15 in order to plan the rest of my year around that day. To say that the opener was sacred is understating my case. In fact, I had pressured and cajoled the Nugent Tribe to organize their schedules to take advantage of this stirring occasion together, and wrangled intensely to make it happen. I was quite proud of myself, for everyone had professional priorities and responsibilities that were not easy to manipulate. But we did it. The few days here in this wonderful setting had produced massive tonnage of grand family memories. The extended time around the fireplace and dinner table was priceless. And no doubt, everyone in attendance needed this important family time together in a big way. Spirits ran high.

Daily guntalk further inspired the primal feelings

all about, and now we were fed, dressed, and psyched to hit the ridges of our sacred huntgrounds before day-light. Dad had his beloved pre-64 Model 70 Winchester in the venerable .300 Savage. Uncle John cradled his custom Remington 700 full of his ultimate 7mm magnum handloads. Johnny slung the sporterized military Springfield '06 over his shoulder. And Jeff thumbed the last of three 7mm magnum rounds into the Browning semi-auto. You could taste the hunt.

More kids drown in buckets of water each year than by gun accidents.

With thermoses and snacks stuffed into pockets and pouches, the redwool brigade was now departing the warmth of Tedquarters for the wilds of nature's most dynamic cycle, the season of harvest. I went into my bedroom to grab the ever important clean handkerchief and a pile of paper napkins. With a light snow still falling, every flake sparkling out my bedroom window in the ambient light of my room lamp, I saw my oily gun rag on my dresser and figured I would wipe the outside of my 7 mag Browning Safari Grade boltgun one last time before venturing into the wetness. Careful to point my "empty" rifle in a safe direction, I poked the muzzle downward at the base of the south wall. Brother Jeff had just walked past me and I remember distinctly watching his feet and legs as I swung the barrel lower so I wasn't

covering anything I wasn't willing to destroy. Also, out
of my peripheral vision I noticed Kevin stroll past the
window just outside in the snowy shadows. Then my
big game gun went POW! Within the confines of the
carpeted, heavy-bedding, insulated, small room, the
shocking sound was at once cacophonous yet muffled.
Oh the mind-numbing power of wishful denial!
Everyone froze. Then it settled in instantly what had
happened, and a black voodoo cloud of fear and confusion enveloped the cabin. Mom came in, then Jeff,
asking "What the hell?!" Dad scowled the look of disciplinarian holy terror. Uncle John confirmed that no one
was hit and patted my shoulder reassuringly. Mike and
Kevin came running to confirm for themselves that the
nightmare scenario hadn't happened. I just stood there
and trembled.

Apparently, sometime in my excited state, I had left
a round in the chamber. As I wiped the bolt area, I must
have inadvertently pulled the trigger and fired the rifle.
But I couldn't remember doing any of these things. I
was a wreck. And I stayed a wreck all day long and well
into the week. Fortunately, the bullet merely ripped a
hole through the base logs of the south wall and harmlessly came to rest in good old terra firma next to the
outside cabin wall. Everyone was supportive and understanding, but we discussed the horrible thing over and

over again to be sure all the gory details sunk into everyone's memory bank. With that misfire forever in mind,
you can bet I'm the hardest ass stickler for gun safety at
every huntcamp I attend!

Those two life-changing events were mind-ruptur-
ing enough to teach me ultra-caution in every gun situation. But the third and—I pray—last uninvited gunpowder
bang in my life was the most devastating negligent discharge that could ever occur this side of losing a life.

Shemane had married me in 1989, what she lovingly refers to as "baptism by fire." We had just finished
putting away the dinner dishes one evening, and she had
started the bathwater for our young son Rocco. I joined
a meeting with our Ted Nugent United Sportsmen of
America staff in the main floor livingroom, and little
Rocco was playing with his army figurines on the master
bedroom floor, upstairs, just a few steps from the bathroom where Shemane was. I could see my son through
the balcony doorway. Our TNUSA staff and I chatted,
in a quiet, comfortable after-dinner way. Then it happened—a sudden, horrifying blast. Surely before the
echo even stopped, I was airborne like a bolt of lightning. I am certain I flew up the flight of twenty or so
stairs in under two seconds. My powerful, loving, pater-
nal instincts were afire like an overreacting mother grizzly. Shemane and I converged on the spot where Rocco

sat upright holding his breath, his tiny five-year-old eyes bugged out twofold. I snatched him up into my arms and Shemane grabbed us both. We did this so swiftly that small white feathers were still floating to the floor from the Bufflehead duck that had just been blasted by a .22-250 Remington Varmint rifle. The duck was one of two mounted side by side above my beautiful, hand-carved wood gun display case next to where Rocco had been playing. Shemane began to cry, Rocco appeared dazed, and I tensed up dramatically with watery eyes myself, out of body.

Once all was secured and we calmed down a bit, we bid good night to our friends and took stock of the horrible fear and confusion that was as tangible in our home as gunsmoke. During our intense investigation of the evidence and crime scene, it was obvious that Rocco had playfully moved his little army men along the steel cable that locked the six long guns together in the open case. The cable not only locked them up, it was strung in and out of the trigger guards to render the guns unloadable, immovable, and inaccessible. Unfortunately and unforgivably, somehow—and to this day we cannot imagine how—that particular rifle actually had a round in the chamber, cocked, with the safety off for God's sake! After much soul-searching and memory-hammering, I am beyond any doubt that I did not put the gun away loaded. We do live in the middle of a wild swamp, and we do occasionally load up a rifle to kill certain varmints that we are obliged to reduce—like raccoons, skunks, possums, wild dogs, wild cats, coyotes, foxes, beavers, and crows. Older son Toby assured us that neither he nor his friends had ever loaded up this particular gun, so we remain stupefied about the matter. Needless to say, that open cabinet is now relegated to the basement for use only during the open deer season, and all unnecessary guns are locked away in safes, virtually inaccessible to any unauthorized individuals. *Especially youngsters.* Call me all the names you wish, for what I, as leader of the household, allowed to transpire is absolutely unforgivable, and I can only thank the Good Lord for saving us from a very close, heart-breaking call. I pray that everybody who reads this will make it a point to make a big deal out of this chapter. Use me as an example of total irresponsibility or do whatever it takes to drive this most unforgivable and unforgettable point home. This last negligent discharge took place more than six years ago, and there have been none since. We remain dedicated and diligent to guarantee that none ever will. ✗

[CHAPTER 27]

THE WHITE ROOM

PEOPLE, ESPECIALLY KIDS, are like mules sometimes. A gentle stroke of the mane, some sugar, and sweet talk can get them into position on occasion, but sometimes ya just gotta whack 'em upside the head with an

I know intuitively how to eliminate nearly all gun problems in America.

oil-soaked two-by-four. So to speak. Ultimately, parents, teachers, and others in authority have to be creative in getting kids' attention. Real, hard-core attention. Had America continued with the quality control of disciplined gun safety education as did our forefathers up through the 1960s, coupled with commonsense law enforcement and a justice system that recognizes something resembling justice, I believe we would not have to be scrambling for such apparent damage control now. Part of this desperate need for last ditch damage control is a result of denying the gun's historical and unavoidable allure. As a boy, I nearly bought the farm through gun foolishness because, even in an actively supervised gun household, I didn't get enough cold blue ballistic action to satisfy my gunsmoke cravings. Learning from that experience, now I know intuitively how to eliminate nearly all gun problems in America. Bold as hell statement, but read on.

On one front, we would all benefit from increased family–gun recreation. The stimulating challenge that is marksmanship discipline would go a long way in bringing families together for more intense quality time. In my opinion, there are no better alternatives. Movies suck for the most part. Television is a subterranean land of bottomfeeders. Spectator sports are just that—not something to do, but rather something to watch others do.

There is no place in America where gun sports aren't available to enjoy. From open state and federal lands, to county gun clubs and public shooting ranges, and of course on the ever loving family farm, no one is more than an hour's drive from a good shootfest. And with all the proper shoot procedures hammered home, nary an accident can be expected. Examine the last ten thousand gun headlines in major daily newspapers across the land. Not one of them occurred on anything resembling a gun range or on a legal gun-outing. They all happened downtown by some paroled puke. Meanwhile, millions upon millions of law-abiding American families are out shooting skeet and trap, hunting, and plinking every weekend all over America, with nary a negligent discharge, injury, or accident to be found.

Quality of life comes from self-discipline augmented with parental discipline.

One of the great joys of shooting with the tribe is that a higher level of awareness, a conscientious discipline, becomes ingrained, appreciated, celebrated. It's a source of great pride that follows through into all aspects of family and individual life. For all practical purposes, Sergeant York can be cloned with a minimum of effort. Through gunsports kids learn the fundamentals for improved excellence in the classroom—like concentration and discipline—as well as for the playground (muscle-control), against peer pressure, and beyond. Rules are cool and details are fun. Quality of life comes from self-discipline augmented with parental and authoritative discipline. That's supervised family shooting fun in a nutshell.

That is all well and good for those inclined to familiarize themselves with firearms and their inherent joys under supervised conditions in current gun families. But the big question is how do we introduce those

young people to Gun Reality 101 who would not otherwise likely be exposed to firearms in a knowledgeable
and responsible fashion? I'll tell you how. Enter "The
White Room."

Implemented into all public and private schools'
mainstream curriculum would be Ballistics 101, from K
through 12th grade. We would find, cultivate, and train
law enforcement officers, retired military personnel, even
qualified volunteers, who can communicate in a proven
effective manner and style to each age group.

At the outset of each school year—just a single day
would suffice—this expert would enter the classroom in
uniform with an uppity, confident, even buoyant spirit
and attitude, carrying a .357 magnum sidearm and a
.223 military longarm. Always smiling, but serious and
direct nonetheless, our expert would address the children in a friendly, workman-like tone and demeanor and
explain how "we are going to learn about guns today."
Holding up an array of different rifle and handgun cartridges, he would cross reference each to an accompanying colorful, large, easy-to-read chart, explaining
relative velocities and kinetic energies in clearly understandable terms. For example, a baseball and hockey
puck's feet-per-second speed in comparison to his .357
and .223 rounds. Ballistic gelatin marked with the corresponding bullet destruction could be fondled and

examined. Various cartridges could be passed around the classroom and questions and answers would follow. We would encourage kids to share their own shooting experiences such as a father's preferred deerhunting round or their own personal experience plinking with a .22. The official in charge could then briefly outline, emphasize, and encourage supervised shooting while coming down hard on any illegal or unsafe anecdote.

A video of TV shooting episodes would be shown exposing them for the folly that they are. It would be explained how thousands of rounds from fully automatic machine guns do not merely cause sparks to fly while no one seems to get hit. Then detailed, graphic photos of actual shooting victims would be reviewed in all their bloody hell as an emphatic display of real world ballistic mayhem. Questions and answers would resume.

Now here's the good part. Enter the never to be forgotten "White Room." The children would be led into a properly constructed prefab shooting range chamber with all white walls, ceiling and floor, with a nice white table at the far end. On the white table would sit six all-white gallon cans of tomato juice with yellow smiley faces on them. The kids would be seated and provided ear and eye protection. The instructor would then put on his ears and eyes, look squarely and sternly into the faces of the children, slam back the bolt of his

AR-15 with the muzzle pointing back at the juice cans. He would then speak in a loud, clear voice, saying, "Pay very close attention, please." At which point he would level the .223 and in a smooth, rapid succession, commence to annihilate three cans in a shower of exploding red juice, splashing violently all over the pretty white walls, table, ceiling and floor, himself, and even some of those in attendance. Slinging the longarm onto his shoulder, our shooter would then unholster his sidearm and do the same to the remaining three cans with the same dynamic results.

Holstering his handgun, he then would turn to face the roomful of stunned kids, fold his arms across his chest, and allow blatant facts to permeate and stain the psyche and souls of everyone there. For the next few moments, the kids would confront the scene and the silence for maximum absorption. I promise you, not one of these children would ever touch a firearm without proper supervision. The commonsense follow up to this bold, brave lesson would be to send home to parents commonsense recommendations on gun safety and information on where to go for shooting lessons so that kids' natural interest and fascination with guns could be channeled in a constructive way.

I am convinced that not only would this powerful experience forcefully deter the misuse of firearms, but, also of equal importance, it would lay the groundwork for an explosion in gun sales and growth in the firearm's industry, perpetuating a dynamic upgrade in responsible firearm ownership. The ultimate result of all this would create a heretofore unprecedented positive voting voice for law-abiding gun owners everywhere. And of course with this increased level of awareness, would come a louder voice for better enforcement of existing gun laws and the elimination of counterproductive laws as well. Simply stated, once "we the people" get more involved, the bureaucrats would scramble to better understand us and, therefore, better represent us. In the absence of sense, nonsense runs amok. 🏹

CHAPTER 28

DEERCAMP

THE FIRST THING I, my family, At deercamp there
and hunt buddies do each year is flip is no stress, no
wildly to the back pages of our new pain, no disease, no
calendars to circle the fifteenth of IRS, no Janet Reno.
November, the traditional opening ————————————
day of Michigan's firearm deer season. At this point, the
remainder of the 364 days falls into place. It is that exciting. All vacation time is nailed for life to coincide with
the rut and the opener. Priorities and enthusiasms. All
souls should have them. Simple, really.

I haven't missed a hunt season in fifty years,
myself. In fact, I've greeted a glowing opening day
shooting light for thirty years straight now, and it is to

that that I owe my sanity, good spirit, balance, and health. Makes for some intense, flamethrowing, rock 'n' roll guitar jamming too. Nature heals, but deercamp is rocket fuel for the fires of life.

Deep in the bigwoods of the Manistee National Forest, inside our dreamy log cabin on the stunning spring-fed lake, Uncle John and Dad sat near the roaring fireplace. Brothers Jeff and Johnny circled the small table with me, all cluttered with guns, ammo, maps, ramrods, cleaning fluid, gun oil, and patches. Wet boots dried on the stoop, red and black wools were draped over the furniture, and an aromatic, bubbling vat of venison chili cooked on the woodstove. While discussing the attributes of pointed soft point bullets and debating the terminal ballistics of the '06 versus .300 Savage versus 7mm mag versus the .270, morning ambush sites were evaluated and contemplated as if life itself depended on the outcome. Two brothers from one generation joined three from another for a timeless celebration of a primal urge, the likes of which cannot be equaled except for maybe welcoming into the world a new family member or saying goodbye to a loved one.

The self-evident truth bestowed upon us by the Creator, "the right to life" means, in it's most simple of terms, getting food hands on to a lot of us. But more important than sustenance for the gut, deercamp and the hunt provide spiritual protein for the soul. Something mystical occurs during the powerful natural season of harvest, and we hunters are irreversibly dedicated to participate, as natural a part of nature as the Northwind herself.

All the sporters I know cannot imagine not hunting. Though each outing surely recreates, and the challenge of outwitting a crafty old buck certainly qualifies as sport, the gathering of the Tribe is, in all its joy, serious business. As we gather under the spell of the campfire, a bonding, open dialogue is inspired. There is no stress, no pain, no disease, no IRS, no Janet Reno. A calm settles all around while, at the same time, we are driven nuts by the intense anticipation of the encounter with the ever mystical symbol of allthings wild—his majesty the deer. Maybe, in our dreams, a really big, smart, huge-racked beast.

I take my kids to all kinds of spectator sport events, skiing, the occasional movie, walking, to dinners, a little shopping, and have always been there for school activities. Those are all very important. But at deercamp a unified focus envelops the family unit, and a combination of individualism and team effort takes on a life of its own that epitomizes what should be, and is, family. Water is carried, wood is stacked, fires are stoked, food is prepared, dishes are washed, and trash is handled.

Little direction is needed, for the obvious cause and effect of the life-support function is clear and evident. Certainly a grand and easily grasped lesson in reality; all but missing in today's crazed and scattered household. Deercamp discipline is mostly *self*-discipline.

Like the intrinsic marksmanship, woodsmanship, and stealth, that all-important deercamp discipline has grown and stayed with me all my life and literally saved me from the death-march that took the lives of so many of my musician friends who lacked those basic lessons. As a father, I glow knowing that my kids are following a steady True North compass founded in fundamental nature lessons that are undeniable in the average deer-camp setting.

I always took my kids hunting, so I've never had to hunt for my kids.

Sure, we have had some sagging buckpoles over the years, and some sparse ones. But if you could hang the trophies of love, respect, care, work ethic, spirit, heart, and soul from a horizontal beam, the Nugent family pole would have crashed to the ground under extreme weight long ago. You see, I always took my kids hunting, so I've never had to hunt for my kids.

With my three eldest mostly grown up now, I cherish the future of the tradition with my ten-year-old son Rocco Winchester. He has shown an excited drive to know wildlife and cultivate his marksmanship and woodslore. He has the eye and the touch. Every kid will respond to the call of nature if given but a small taste. That tiny seed, in many cases, will flourish into an out and out conservation mindset that will motivate them to no end. I'm fifty-two now and crave it more than ever. As goes the quality of wildground to provide these deer-camp experiences, so goes the source of our quality of life, for critter habitat is only as good as the air, soil, and water quality it provides. That's quality of life any way you cut it.

Deercamp is powerful medicine. And its future is worth fighting for. The electric, romantic sensations derived from each day there should remind us to keep that spirit alive in between hunt seasons. Uncle John and Dad are gone now. So are Fred, George, Whitey, and Stan. But I can close my eyes with only the stimulating flavor of the oakfire smoke to remind me of the moving lessons they all taught me throughout our deercamps together. And I know I must do all I can to keep their spirit alive. I shall. I must.

The smoke drifts up, southeast, gently across the lake, and I know that Dad would have told me to hit the lee side of the white oak saddle. There I can catch the deer moving in from the northwest ridge on their way to the sawgrass marsh. I'll take Rocco there, and we will not be alone. Deercamp comes alive on Wednesday this year. We will begin again. We are excited.

CHAPTER 29

UP NORTH

THE WORDS "UP NORTH" res-
onate throughout the Nugent household, and all of Michigan, like a call to
arms for warriors of the wild. Ever
since the thrilling fall voyages up I-75
in the family station wagon in the
1950s, I have looked forward to an

Mother Nature
supplies all the
thrills a family
could want. There
is never a dull
moment.

annual northbound trip. No matter how crazed and
stressful the modern world gets, these excursions never
fail to deliver a satisfying and relieving adventure for the
whole tribe. Though there is nothing quite like a fall
hunting trip into the big timber country with that
intense season of harvest's cool air, our summer trips get
better every year. There is so much to do in the North

Country that every member of the family looks forward to something fun and exciting.

It all begins with the decision to head out. Packing bags and loading up the big Suburban is a kick unto itself. I don't know what I would do without this over-sized SUV. Bows and arrows, guns, fishing gear, ball, bat, gloves, soccer ball, football, dogs, kennels, duffel bags, wildlife feed, bikes, a huge cooler, groceries, and enough stuff to equip a small army is packed carefully by every-one together. Shared chores make for a neat team effort and increases the anticipation overall. The hounds have figured out exactly what all the commotion is about over the years and they instinctively know they are joining us for a journey into the wilds of Up North. We all bark and howl with joy!

Michigan isn't the only Up North celebration state. Wisconsin, Minnesota, Pennsylvania, and New York use this eternal colloquialism as well. So many Ohioans and Indiana families have come to love their time in Michigan's wild North Country that they, too, use the catchy phrase. We are after all the winter, water wonder-land state, and we welcome everybody.

When we cruise north we try to slow down and experience all the beautiful scenery of our state. Books and maps are referenced to appreciate the grand history of Michigan for the kids. Different routes are planned to see and learn more each trip. The road less traveled seems to provide a more relaxed drive. We buckle up and take it easy, challenging each other to identify points of interest. It is a great education for everybody. You can feel the stress dissipating immediately. No headphones, electronic games, or distractions for us. There is always something to see, and wildlife sightings are the big bonus. Every mile produces different species of hawks, a plethora of birdlife, waterfowl, squirrels, and the ever present whitetail deer, the official state mammal. Mother Nature supplies all the thrills a family could want. There is never a dull moment.

Though the pace is calming and easy-going, we nonetheless maintain a reasonable schedule to make the trip efficient. We pee before we depart and on gas or rest stops only. That is rule #1. The dogs need a couple of relief breaks so we capitalize on these essential pit stops for a welcome stretch. Only healthy snacks are packed for overall comfort and pleasant drive time. And it is a felony to ask if we are there yet.

Recently we reveled in the glory of the magnificent Manistee National Forest. So many lakes, streams, rivers, and ponds to swim, canoe, and fish make for a dynamic choice of adventurezones. Michigan has more public access grounds and water than any state east of the Mississippi, and we take full advantage of this cornucopia of opportunities. The cities of Manistee, Ludington, Cadillac, Traverse City, and so many other small towns offer unlimited quality food, lodging, and fun. The people Up North are a friendly, courteous breed of Americans, and their warm, generous hospitality makes one feel right at home. We've eaten at Blondie's Diner and Mivernas in Traverse City and had delicious chow. The River Walk Cafe in Manistee grills up the best burgers we have ever enjoyed. A morning of archery at Gauthiers in Traverse City sharpens the eye for the upcoming bowhunting season.

On one particular trip, north of Traverse City in the small town of Central Lake, the whole family had a riot shooting machine guns at the Second Chance Body Armor national law enforcement shoot out. Now that's fun. Full auto fun. Young Rocco and his buddy Thompson shot a .50 caliber Browning military tripod-mounted machine gun as well as an old .45 caliber Tommygun. There is always something special to do if you just ask around or call the tourist bureau of your designated vacation area. Charter fishing is always an adventure, and the fishing has never been better.

Go north, my friends, every chance you get. Up North will cleanse the soul. All year long. Pack the essential travel safety supplies like first aid kits, a fire extinguisher, food and water, a blanket, and a cell phone if you can. Take it easy, plan ahead, BUCKLE UP—DON'T BE ROADKILL—and breathe the clean air and drink the good water. Let Mother Nature be your guide and watch the family get happier and closer. Maybe I'll see you sometime in Grayling at the Grayling Restaurant where Fred Bear and I used to eat cherry pie and drink cold milk. Up North will always be Fred Bear country. In the wind, he's still alive. ⚚

CHAPTER 30

TRIBE NUGE—GIVING THANKS TO THE GREAT SPIRIT

GOOD TRADITIONS can drive a man's soul. Standard annual activities introduced to us from birth will guide a young person's life, but once we survive our teenage years we should probably question anything and everything *status quo*. After all, slavery was a tradition of sin for many years, and good riddance to all bad habits. But as I raise my family for optimum quality of life, I encourage them all to intellectually review everything and anything that life has to offer, making the smart decision to do the right thing. Rosa Parks is my hero. And there was and sadly remains today, to a pathetic degree, a tradition of substance abuse all around me in my music industry, my beloved

> Once we survive our teenage years we should probably question anything and everything status quo.

hunting community, and elsewhere. But to hell with foolishness. True North is not always easy, but it's always best.

As my children grow, I cherish any and all opportunities for us to gather together. Parenting never ends. The hunting season has always been a time of return for Tribe Nuge and represents a tradition of family celebration for us that becomes more important each year. No matter how crazy and hectic our lives may be, we do whatever it takes to spend as much time together as possible in the glorious fall. Especially on ThanksGiving weekend.

I thank the Good Lord all year long for the health and happiness of our clan living here in the last best place on earth, and I take extra care to lovingly pressure my older kids, brothers, sister, and their families to sit with each other at the stacked dinner table on this traditional day and look to the heavens with sincere appreciation for the awesome sustenance from the good Mother Earth. It is essential to do so during the actual season of harvest from which we derive our life's protein and yum. There is no denial of the perfection of nature when a thinking man dines from her abundance.

Sustenance is our target; health and balance in the wild is our goal.

Out our lakeside home windows as we toast the Spirit, the flying, honking flights of Canada geese that join us are a powerful reminder of our relationship with the Great Spirit. Like the venison, turkey, and wild goose on our table, alongside the various delicious fibrous chow, there is no hiding that from death comes life, and the cycle must be respected and never broken. Yowsa, yowsa, and pass the natural grits.

There's a solid reason why ThanksGiving is celebrated in November. In 1621, after more than half the new American pilgrims had perished for lack of food and shelter the previous winter, a deerhunting party was organized to supplement a good crop of Indian corn and barley. Indian Chief King Massasoit and Governor William Bradford declared a day of ThanksGiving by leading a prayer to God and the Great Spirit. Officially in 1777, following the surrender of British Major General Burgoyne, the Continental Congress declared the first national proclamation, "that with one heart and one voice, the good people may express the grateful feelings of their hearts, and consecrate themselves, to the service of the Divine benefactor...." See, I may be just a guitar player, but I knew it all along that these powerful celebrations and festivities were about hunting and the right to keep and bear arms, separate yet one.

And so goes another fine tradition, that the bow and arrow is swapped for the scoped shotgun on this day. A preferred methodology has been continued where I open the gun season with firepower, then switch back to

bowhunting 'til ThanksGiving Day. I have no real expla-
nation except that I just plain love guns, long-range
marksmanship, and the smell of gunpowder whenever I
can get it. Opening day of firearm deer season is a powerful human experience, let me tell ya. ThanksGiving
Day is, too. I toss and turn all night in bed like a kid on
Christmas Eve expecting a new bike and a gun.

I remember one particular ThanksGiving morning, we all had lotsa action with many deer encountered
by everybody. Many shots were heard on the adjoining
properties and excitement was in the air. We didn't take
a deer in our party but spirits were running high
enough, that's for sure. The atmosphere could not have
been more conducive for a wonderful midday family
meal. We were giddy. And we ate like we appreciated it.

With about three hours of good shooting light
remaining, we trooped into the big swamp for round
two. I chose a traditional hogback ridge overlooking the
Northswamp, but within sight of the house and horse-
barn. Approaching my set a little differently than usual,
I chose to hang my sniper shotgun on a hook above me
in my 16-foot ladderstand and hang onto my bow,
hoping for an archery kill this afternoon. I have always
picked one or the other, figuring that the indecision
between two weapons would certainly foul up a fleeting

crack at the big buck if he were to ever show up. But with the increased advantage of elevation in this tall ladder on this high ridge and the vast visibility provided, I felt confident I could pull it off. A ridgerunner could be bowbagged and a marshbuck would be mine out to 200 yards with the Sniper Browning 12. And it's legal, what the hell.

The dark, overcast skies were like an old good friend, and I was warm and snug in my heavy, traditional red and black wools with the added warmth of the incredible Carol Davis longjons. I had much to be thankful for. Brother Jeff loved this set, and son Toby staked out the west ridge further on. The rut in Southern Michigan is usually well over or at least winding down by ThanksGiving, but within an hour a small, 6-point buck came crashing out of the tamaracks hot on the tail of a big she-deer, nostrils flaring, raising hell. They scrambled right under my set, offering an easy shot at the little buck, but, hoping that he might travel past my brothers or the kids, I let 'em go. And that's never easy for this old boy, let me tell ya. But as I nurture young son Rocco Winchester into more hunting, I find myself getting real selective and patient. It's about time.

The wind picked up and more does came and went in and out of the open marsh around me. Two more pretty nice 8-points followed the bottom of the ridge that offered easy shotgun shots, but I still had my bow in my hands, hoping.

With a slight rustle and a premonition, I glanced behind me into the timberline and the decision to grab the shotgun was immediate. A huge, gorgeous, white-racked beast was strutting my way from the oaks hot on the tail of a huge doe. He would run with his head to the ground, stop, swing his mature Roman nose all around, then get right back on the old gal, coming on strong.

I almost fumbled and dropped my bow to the ground, I was so excited, but managed to snag the Browning and hang my bow in time to twist into shooting position. And none too soon, as Beasto Boy stopped and looked clean through me from 100 yards into the saw-grass. Yikes! I froze momentarily in half-ready position, then slowly brought the shotgun the final 2 inches to my shoulder. The Leupold scope came right up to perfect eye relief like it had on a thousand practice sessions, and the safety snicked off in one fluid move. The second the duplex crosshairs crossed the buck's shoulder my right hand squeezed the grip and the trigger like I was squeez-ing lemon juice on bluegill filets, and the big 12 ROARED! All I saw when I came out of the slight recoil of the automatic was a white belly against the black muck and beige reeds. The big, heavy 8-pointer was down for the count. The doe looked on nonchalantly then slowly picked her way into no-man's land.

I studied him for a minute or two in the scope with the safety off just to make sure, but he was not going anywhere. The awesomely destructive Remington hollowpoint copper slug had smashed both of his shoulders and everything in between to smithereens, and killed him instantly. An amazing round, to be sure. I leaned back hard against my giant oak trunk and whooshed out a big gulp of air. WOW! Happy ThanksGiving y'all.

My best hunting partner, son Toby, helped me load the huge mature buck into the big gamebasket of our Honda four-wheeler, but we had some trouble. He was truly one of the largest deer I had ever taken and created way too much weight in the back of the ATV. When I attempted to wheel up the ridge, his massive weight caused the unit to wheelstand dramatically and tipped over backwards, almost taking me out. Wouldn't the animal rights geeks have loved that? But justice prevailed, and we reloaded and remaneuvered with Toby sitting up front for balance. When we weighed the beast, the scales hammered 239 pounds dead weight. YOWSA, I say. Big boy, indeed. His antlers were gorgeous with eight even points, tall, heavy, and wide. His G-2 on the left side was 11 inches long, and we rough scored him around 155 B&C inches, my best gunbuck ever.

I sure know where I am going to have son Rocco or Toby hunt next ThanksGiving—heck, maybe the three of us together. Some traditions are so grand and so good that we must celebrate them more and aggressively pass them on. This emotionally moving culture of hunting and heritage, at its spiritual peak on ThanksGiving Day, may be the most powerful reminder of all we can share with our children. We're already giving immense thanks as we speak. The tradition lives on at Camp Nugent.

As families in touch with the good Mother Earth wrap up the natural season of harvest, it is only fitting to sit down together, look to the heavens, connect hands and hearts, and show appreciation and sincere thanks for the life-giving sustenance that comes from hard work and a thriving resource stewardship. Renewable resources mean food. Food for the body and the spirit.

Tribe Nuge, along with millions of American hunting families and others, get giddy around a table full of pure, delicious natural food in the form of wildfowl, venison, wild turkey, quail, dove, pheasant, grouse, woodcock, squirrel, rabbit, and a multitude of wonderful, organic, high-protein chow.

The house is aflutter with laughter and joyful activity as grandmas, grandpas, aunts, uncles, moms, dads, sons, daughters, grandkids, and hunting dogs run amok. Everybody lends a helping hand as plate after steaming plate of delectable chow is spread across the table. Sweet smelling haunch of smoked venison and succulent, golden brown wild turkey is the usual main course with potatoes, yams, squash, turnips, beans, home baked bread, and pumpkin pie from scratch, plus other precious foods drooled over by all in attendance. Hands are held and a prayer of serious thanks is offered up for the bounty of the natural fall harvest.

At Camp Nugent and in the more than sixty million hunting and fishing families' homes across America, a vivid and powerful connection with the good Mother Earth and her life-giving renewable resources comes to dynamic fruition. Those of us who hunt our own food have a deep and abiding reverence for this natural sustenance we stalk and kill ourselves. It is on the sacred wildgrounds of the hunt that we monitor and respond to habitat considerations and the very health and condition of the wildlife that brings us thrills afield and food for the table.

Eating and sharing the productivity from a proper hands-on harvest with family and friends emphasizes our unavoidable cause and effect and resultant logical obligation to the Good Earth and all her glorious resources. Actually taking part in the equation of sustain-yield management strongly reinforces our awareness of the pressures we all place on the environment.

That's why I have always understood how vital a role hunting, fishing, and trapping has played in the overall scheme of conservation and ecology awareness.

And that is why Tribe Nuge, when gathered around the table, always gives special thanks for our uniquely American liberty and the hunt. We also give an appreciable nod to the great farmers of the land for their hard work and stewardship and for providing food for the masses of the world. But know, too, that many in the ag-community prefer the bounty of the wild harvest more so. As modern man scrambles to return to the healing qualities of nature, we hunters smile and nod, knowing that so many of us never left her side. The Physics of Spirituality that is the hunting lifestyle is more intense now than at any time in history, for today the stress of the concrete jungle takes more of a toll than the threat of the saber-toothed tiger of yore—at least he just killed you outright.

So give a toast to the Great Spirit and to the modern huntclan, standing shoulder to shoulder, haunch to haunch, heart to heart, thankful that our joint efforts have managed game animals to their healthiest, most thriving condition in recorded history. More fresh, delicious, low-fat, high-protein, E. coli–free venison and pure, free-range, salmonella-free wildfowl is being consumed than ever before. A short few hundred years ago, the original American hunting tribes invited their guests to the table-o-harvest and we are very proud that the tradition of giving and thanks soars on.

Sustenance is our target; health and balance in the wild is our goal. We have achieved both, and with recent hunting seasons being the safest ever all over America, we live to do it again. No bird is more wonderful than the wild turkey encountered at dawn under a gunmetal spring sky. No flesh more pure than the magnificent deer in the forest, with crowspeak and wildsong resonating in your heart.

I thank God for the bounty. I thank God for the rain on my face and the giant oak tree that holds my treestand. I thank God I can taste, smell, hear, see, and climb. I thank Him for the feelings I experience every time I leave the pavement behind and connect with His creation. I thank my dad, Uncle John, and Fred Bear for teaching me to be a good hunter. I thank my mom for encouraging me to work hard at my archery and marksmanship. I thank my wife Shemane for letting me hunt every day of the season. I thank my kids for putting up with their outdoor-addicted old man. I thank Browning for a balanced, pointable gun. I thank Winchester for Bismuth shot to fill my bag with ducks. I thank God for Labrador retrievers. I thank my fellow hunters and dedicated biologists in the Department of Natural

Resources and other state wildlife agencies for standing up for common sense, honesty, and our incredibly successful wildlife management heritage. And I thank God every day for the stunning critters that bring us so much joy, excitement, and perfect food for the table. I thank the Founding Fathers of America for writing down self-evident truths and the lessons of abuse at the hands of tyrants and monsters, so we can live in the last and only best place. I thank so many editors for letting me represent the sport community with writings of politically incorrect reality. I thank Gibson for the loudest and sexiest guitars in the world. And I thank my upbringing in the MotorCity Madhouse for all the precious attitude and spirit. I thank Walt Disney for the Bambi cartoon and the illogical fantasy nonsense it inspired to create the laughable antihunters to further the common sense that hunting always has been and always will be. ThanksGiving is really a state of mind. Everyday.

CHAPTER 31

HOW TO INSPIRE A CHILD INTO THE WILD

MY DAD WAS A HUNTER when I was born in 1948. It was still a powerful, natural, commonsense, American way of life back then. Dad really enjoyed his quiet, peaceful bowhunting time afield and made it a point to share it with his family. He had quit gun hunting by the time I was ten because of a terrible firearm accident that almost killed him. Some dufus had touched off a round from his Winchester M94, 30-30 levergun while unloading it in the back seat of a '52 Ford coupe and nearly took my dad's head clean off. Another inch, and I would have been a single-parent kid. Mindless, idiotic

All life comes from beyond the pavement and our call to stewardship of these precious life-giving renewable resources runs strong and deep.

NEGLIGENCE is still the only way to be injured or die from a gun "accident." He stressed this to us, making it a point to clearly differentiate *accidents* from *negligence*. I thank him for that to this day.

But it was the adventure of our Up North family treks each fall that fanned the flames of my predatory and conservation spirit. It was the bigwoods of the North Country and the occasional sighting of all wildlife, small and big game—especially the majestic, always elusive whitetail deer—that brought me much adrenaline dumpage. Each sound, sight, smell, and feeling beyond the pavement zinged straight into my heart and soul. I needed very little motivation from anyone or anything outside my own interests in animals and habitat. The woods, rivers, fields, and the wind called my name clearly.

The young mind you help guide to TRUE NORTH now will be the warrior for the wild his or her entire life.

Growing up along the wildground of the River Rouge outside Detroit, my fascination with wildlife and hunting was something that could not be defused. I was hooked. Something about the dynamics of each critter encounter drove me wild. The fact that my dad was already experimenting with this brand-new bowhunting concept was just an added kicker. My river stalking days with slingshot and bow and arrow imprinted deeply into my psyche from day one, and between my dad, Uncles John and Dick, and Fred Bear, I had all the role modeling a kid could ask for.

It is interesting to note that my brothers Jeff and John and younger sister Kathy, though a part of every hunting trip and outing, showed no more than a passing interest in the sport. We all had grand times together learning about family camplife and nature lessons, but they could, quite frankly, take it or leave it. Meanwhile, I plunged into the wild at every opportunity. Every day after school, while the other kids were playing ball sports, tag, hide-n-seek, or so many other normal kid's games, I was stalking the riverbanks trying to get close to pheasant, quail, ducks, squirrels, possum, coons, skunks, rabbits, and all sorts of birds and other wildlife. There was a marshy area at the riverbend we called Skunk Hollow. I knew every wonderful mucky inch of the place.

So what is the difference between one kid and another, when all experiences might be basically the same, that drives one to hunt but not the other? Many moms and dads across the country have asked me how to get their kids interested in hunting, and I can only tell them what my own experiences have shown. My best hunting buddies are my own two sons, twenty-three-year-old Toby and ten-year-old Rocco. They accompany me on many outings, and we have shared many powerful

moments together seeking game. But there was no for-
mula that I adhered to. Rather, it is a deeply ingrained—
and, therefore, spontaneous—process to optimize the
chances that they would pursue this outdoor lifestyle
with me that has brought me so much enjoyment, excitement, happiness, and gratification. All life comes from
beyond the pavement, and our call to stewardship of
these precious life-giving renewable resources runs
strong and deep. For if a father fails to bring these lessons
of reality and elements of accountability into his family's
life, what good has he accomplished?

Certainly, my exhilaration upon merely seeing
game is contagious. I have made it a point to raise my
family on wonderful, game-rich wildground, thereby
maximizing the sightings that can be shared and talked
about together. The first word out of each of my kid's
mouths was "deer," as they pointed out the window or
along a trail together with Mom and Dad. Watching
wildlife shows on TV together as a family and exploring
easy-access wildground as often as possible brings the
dynamic of wildlife encounters to the forefront of children's young minds. As wildlife habitat faces the growing curse of development and destruction, these
beyond-the-pavement areas for introduction are becoming harder and harder to find and access. This is why
efforts and programs to save wildground are so impor-

tant today. Join Ducks Unlimited, Rocky Mountain Elk Foundation, Pheasants Forever, Trout Unlimited, Quail Unlimited, and any other organization you can afford. Habitat progress is job one!

Most important, I did not push my children to hunt. I always made it available to them, gently prodding and encouraging them to join me every time I went afield but never to the point of force or pressure. I shared the thrills of each and every hunt in stories and photos and made it a point to let them know every night at the dinner table, "You should have been there! It was really cool!"

Over the years, I tried to get them to join me on the easier maneuvers. Break them in gently. Comfortable temperatures and conditions were always more alluring than stormy, wet, cold, and nasty mornings in the duck-blind! But I did make it a point to let them experience the joys of Ma Nature's wrath as well. There is nothing more wonderful than coming back to a warm, cozy cabin, lodge, or tent; wet, cold, and beat; changing into fresh, dry clothes; and sipping a steaming bowl of soup or chili around a roaring fireplace or campfire. That is heaven on earth, and everybody enjoys it immensely. They always gaze into the fire and hear the call.

As my children grow up they spend more and more time hunting with their dear old dad. Toby and I have a duck opener ritual that means the world to me. And Rocco and I sneak up the same ridge at daybreak every September 15, opening day of squirrel season. Toby loves packing into elk camp, and the whole family looks forward to our annual African safari. I can't really enjoy a hunt for more than a week if my clan is not with me. I feel unfulfilled and I get homesick for them.

I read a story in the American Airlines *American Way* magazine recently about a successful executive's attempt to connect with his son by taking him on a hunting trip, much to the boy's protest. The old man ended up arguing with his son, hunting alone, then opting to take a big buck's photo instead of killing it, as if this merciful gesture would somehow bring him closer to his son. BALDERDASH! It was even clearly articulated in the story how overpopulated and destructive the deer were in northern Illinois, the scene of the episode, and the desperate and essential need to reduce the herd responsibly. It did, however, fail miserably in detailing the truth about habitat needs and the fundamental function of man and beast, balancing their natural roles in the inescapable cycle of life and death. His "non-consumptive" gesture was denial in action and plain wrong.

Contrary to this politically correct pap, bold, honest lessons in life's cycle of reality will connect deeply with a young child. Be sure to read the wildlife reports from scientific publications and note relative observations when driving the highways. Watch the Discovery Channel nature specials together and never let fantasy or denial become acceptable. Show your love and passion for the outdoors, and it will be contagious. I see it all the time, not only with young boys but equally with little girls, too. Now that's a thrill!

If your kid spends more than thirty minutes a day in front of the TV set or plays zombie-inducing video games, you are asking for trouble. If you can't remember the last Saturday you took the family to a wild place, early and long, you are asking for trouble. If you can't talk with your kids because they have headphones glued to their ears, you are out of their loop, and may I dare say, a failing parent. If you don't have quality time discussing the little things in your lives together at the dinner table each night you are missing out on one of the most powerful opportunities to connect that there is.

Hunting the fine state of Texas each year for many years, I have come to greatly appreciate their laws encouraging parents to take young children hunting. You see, Texas has the very best laws regarding minimum ages for hunting. THERE IS NO MINIMUM AGE! It is a proven fact that if a child does not hunt by the time he or she is nine or ten, it is unlikely that he or she will ever pursue an outdoor life. That is catastrophic. Every year in Texas I meet families that enjoy hunting together with four-, five-, and six-year-olds who kill deer with rifles at these young ages. No accidents. No injuries. No problems. With a custom fitted .223, 6mm, or .243, these little whippersnappers take deer cleanly and regularly.

Just like the scientists and medical community now admit, responsible parenting begins in the womb. Nightly bedsongs, gentle readings, loving talk from both parents and siblings forms a prebirth bond that will most certainly connect with this new life. It is never too early.

THERE IS NO GREATER RESPONSIBILITY THAN PARENTING! Period.

Immediately after birth there is an initial explosion of brain synapses. Synaptic connections continue powerfully through adolescence, according to a recent study from the University of Chicago. The experts generally agree that if this initial touch is lost or not fully taken advantage of, strong learning influences can be made up for later. Some areas of the brain such as the prefrontal cortex, where higher thought, reasoning, judgment, and motivation come from, will be best molded by a parent's loving touch throughout adolescence. BUT, a really good parent wouldn't miss out on any of these opportunities to provide the most positive conditions possible for his child.

And according to this old dad, it never stops. The time to share the excitement of the wild with your kids is NOW! The earlier, the better. The most meaningful impact will be made in their first five years. My mind burns with graphic excitement envisioning my family's woodland walks, riverbank picnics, sunrise celebrations, and wildlife encounters with bow and arrow or .22 rifle in hand. Be sure to make that extra effort to conduct those ever-so-valuable wild lessons out there beyond the pavement for the entire family as often as you can. Earmark special weekends. Pack a lunch and a camera. Go slow. Take it all in. Nature will do the rest.

Provide nature-oriented toys and learning materials. Share your enthusiasm for the wild. If you are going to rent videos, rent quality hunting and wildlife tapes and watch along, reviewing the statements and content for details and better understanding.

Other reports show how children who have had little or no meaningful touch with mom and/or dad are much more likely to lead a life of crime, substance abuse, unfulfilled sadness, and often a horrible, tragic early death. To know the remedy for this tragedy yet fail to respond is the worse sin of mankind.

The young mind you help guide to TRUE NORTH now will be the warrior for the wild his or her entire life. I'll bet on it.

With simple, good parenting fueled by good old-fashioned love and affection, you will develop the greatest hunting partner you could ever ask for. The wild needs the next generation, and the next generation needs the wild. Strong and free.

SO TAKE A YOUNGSTER INTO THE WILD AS SOON AND AS OFTEN AS YOU CAN. GET 'EM SHOOTING, EXPLORING, AND THROBBING. NOW! 🏹

CHAPTER 32

EVERY FATHER'S DREAM

1 ADMIT 1T. I'm an addicted braggart. Seems no matter with whom, where, or when, I am compelled to talk about my kids. My eldest daughter Starr has organized the American dreamlife with a hard workin', loving, caring hubby and given me the most beautiful granddaughter any gramps could ever ask for. Sasha has managed our family Ted Nugent United Sportsmen of America crusade to make my heart soar and is the most loving, giving, caring, level-headed, gutsy little girl to ever shine a father's smile. Son number one is right up there in the asset column as well. Toby managed the TNUSA shipping department, is a world-class athlete, is on his way to

> The Spirit of the Wild forges a great father-son bond that teaches all you need to know about the good things in life.

becoming a professional model, and would give you the shirt off his back. He's a man's man and gave me my greatest fatherly thrill of a lifetime when he killed the biggest whitetail buck in Nugent Tribe history last season. He's my best hunting buddy.

But it all came into digital technicolor focus today as the sun rose over our northridge above the reedmarsh, and my youngest son Rocco and I sat at the base of an old white oak tree together, taking it all in. Rocco's acute hearing guided me toward the incoming goose music and the distant mallard speak. We winked knowingly at each other as big acorns rained down upon our wild domain, eagle-eyeing the towering canopy for squirrel action, .22 rifles cradled across our knees. In whispered tones he asked me what birdsong belonged to what bird, and if I did this when I was a kid, too. We reviewed all the safety details over and over again just like my dad did with me forty years ago. I felt so wonderfully and completely fatherly as he peppered me with question after question about elephant guns and old birddogs, slingshots and BB guns, red squirrels and fox squirrels, chipmunks and crows, .22 shorts vs. long rifles. My dad-badge glowed that I could answer them all.

We took a moment to double-check the zero of his little Chipmunk .22 rifle, and I sighed inward relief as he blasted a small chip of wood to pieces, square on. I tried to congratulate him matter-of-factly, attempting to hide my overwhelming glee in hopes of not overdoing it. The Spirit of the Wild forges a great father–son bond that teaches all you need to know about the good things in life.

On one memorable father–son excursion into the wilderness, Rocco Winchester squirmed into the thick cedarbush. The Ruger .223 rifle firmly in his grasp, he lay prone in the brisk, December, Texas air. His gaze intense, his heartbeat a thumpin', a long, deep, calculated breath exhaled slowly into the dirt as his trigger finger began the disciplined squeeze that his old man had taught him for the always thrilling marksmanship challenge. The deep, guttural "caw-caw crrrr" of a big black raven directly overhead punctuated the primeval atmosphere that enveloped this young boy and his father. This ain't no Nintendo stroke goin' on here. We're talking the real McCoy of sensual stimuli and adrenaline-pumping articulation of the mind, body, and soul. That is no video image in the crosshairs of his riflescope. That's a real, live, wary, custom-designed-for-maximum-escape, flesh-and-blood whitetail deer yonder, kids, and he's coming our way. The heart begins to sound like a Tommy Aldridge double bassdrum solo gone illegally ballistic, about to punch clean outta the chest. And it feels damn good. At this young age, Rocco isn't all that sure exactly what is taking place inside, but he's sure of one thing; it feels cool as hell, and he loves it. For certain, it's timeless and pure.

I do my best to keep silent and let my son make his own decisions, though my own heart is racing out of control too. All my dutiful parenting and instructions have already taken place over the years we trained and practiced together. Now, as in life, he had to call on his own wits and intellect, a real, no excuses sense of cause and effect, to be individually responsible for the outcome. If only the rest of modern life were so pure.

But Rocco gets it. He knows that venison feeds his family. He knows that it is better food. He knows the deer can get away, and usually does. He knows he must think and think hard, the whole time remaining calm, motionless, and in control. Sounds like the kind of stuff all kids should learn, doesn't it? IT IS!

With a slight adjustment of his headphone hearing protectors, I watch his muscles relax and I can feel it about to happen. The boy is under some serious pressure right now because only an hour earlier he had flinched from an uncertain rifle rest position and missed a dandy 8-pointer by a mile. He was visibly upset. Ol' dad consoled him lovingly, and we worked through it together. But now, he was determined. Locked. In the zone. He had told me in disgust how he didn't follow

the rules and breathe easy and squeeeeeeze on that earlier shot, and he was committed to doing it right this
time. I was proud already.

And POW! He did. The handsome two-and-a-half-
year-old trophy 8-point buck slammed to the ground
without a twitch, the high velocity bullet devastating
both lungs and heart, killing him instantly. Unbelievable!
Time stood still.

With Dad doing all he could to hold the video
camera steady, Rocco was taped cautiously approaching
his prize, rifle at the ready, with a smile that stretched all
the way back to San Antonio. He was ultra-pumped.
Gaga-eyed, we examined the beautiful animal. Together
we stroked the sleek, grey, smooth hollow hairs of his
winter coat. We each grabbed a handful of majestic,
regal antler, and held his head high, looking at every
angle in awe. We sat back on the cold, rock-hard Texas
ground, and with a stunning gold-orange sunset-aug-
mented glow highlighting the dynamic beast and the
graphic, unforgiving Texas landscape, we just fell silent.

We dragged the buck into the shade of the thick
scrub, and settled into our makeshift hideout for the last
hour of daylight. Amazingly, and only in Texas, could it
happen; forty minutes later, the same scenario unfolded
for another climactic shot on yet another beautiful 8-
point buck. My nine-year-old son had just tagged his

second trophy whitetail in a single evening. A sense of disbelief permeated the two of us.

At his age, I can only imagine his thoughts, but mine were rocking. I knew he admired the obvious beauty of the animals and the land. I knew he was plenty aware of the awesome design of God's mystifying creation. Certainly Rocco was very proud of his patience and all the discipline that he put into his shot preparation. Was he thinking of the great meat for our table? Was he conscience of the battles that lay ahead of him to safeguard the very nature of this dynamic experience? Was he cognizant of those anti-nature extremists who would outlaw this pure occurrence in the name of animal rights? Or was he just celebrating father, son, and nature without the vacuous baggage of political correctness? His ever growing smile and sparkling eyes told the whole story. It was all good.

Roll after roll of carefully directed photos were taken, and shortly thereafter, his mother rode up with our Y.O. Ranch guide, Vick Jones. The celebration started all over again. It was joyous and remains so forever.

CHAPTER 33

MY SON, THE DEERHUNTER

LITTLE SASHA WAS ONLY eight years old as she slithered up to the dilapidated barbed wire fence. We ignored the chilling Texas air that December evening, for father and daughter were sneaking up on a big old southwest whitetail doe. Younger brother Toby kept up with us in the tall grass clumps of the rimrock, and we made it to the fence line undetected. After years of practicing with their scoped Crossman pellet rifle in the livingroom, I knew these kids could shoot, and in the thinking state of Texas young kids are encouraged to hunt with their families. Just as my baby snicked the safety off the Remington .22 and settled in for the shot,

Hunting and firearm marksmanship is the greatest discipline for youngsters.

———————————

I saw the glint of antlers emerge from the scrub. I nudged her and pointed like a quaildog on a covey as she swung the little rifle onto the now standing buck. I was about to remind her to squeeze when the gun cracked and the 9-point buck tipped over 100 yards away.

I remember it like it was yesterday. Not only for the great experience we shared together and the celebration of a true trophy whitetail by my little girl, but also for the deer that Toby missed that trip. He didn't like that one bit, and I know it has haunted him all these years. I take my parenting very seriously, and I always do my best to encourage excellence in my children. Hunting and firearm marksmanship is the greatest discipline for youngsters. Even though I am addicted to allthings outdoors, I have never pushed my kids to hunt, but rather, shared my love of the wild with them and always encouraged them to join me.

Toby is every father's dream son. Smart, caring, loyal, honest, independent, generous, downright good-looking, and always thinking of others. I love him with all my heart, and he is a great hunter in his own right. He's expertly bagged bear, caribou, and awesome African game with his bow and arrows, and our annual duck opener is a sacred ritual. He's a natural. But the deer have always evaded him. 'Til now.

Sighting in the Browning 12-gauge slug gun showed his natural hand-eye touch and his patience was proven with some long vigils over the years. His buddy Brad got the bug from hanging 'round the contagious Nugent huntzone, and now the two friends decided they would give it a go in the big Northswamp this cool fall evening. I had been saving an area for just such an occasion and instructed the intrepid Natty Bumpos to their positions. I took my bow to the east and settled in for the stimulifest that every hour in the wild produces.

Within moments of strapping on my safety belt, gunfire echoed to the north. I grinned broadly, knowing the thrill at hand of the deer encounter my son was wallowing in. It took everything I had not to get down to investigate. Then within fifteen minutes a pair of shots rang out from Brad's location, just as a little buck stopped barely out of bowrange from me. Eventually the young deer moved under my tree stand, and a double lunger brought him to bag cleanly. Venison was ours!

With darkness falling, I raced to the barn where Toby and Brad stood smiling wildly over Brad's handsome 4-pointer.

"I heard you shoot, Toby! Where's yours?" I asked.

Through a painfully uncontrollable ear to ear grin, Toby tried to tell me he had missed, but Brad couldn't stand it and yelled out, "He killed the beast!" There, around the corner of the barn, lay the epitome of his whitetailness! A magnificent eleven-point monster with heavy, thick, tall, wide sweeping antlers that all hunters dream of. With an awesome 130-yard slugshot through the lungs, Toby had ended his fifteen year wait for his first deerkill. It was a spectacular moment for us all. I lunged for the deer and grabbed his stunning horns in my hands, heaving to lift the huge 250-pound venison torso, demanding to hear every minute detail of the encounter and the shot. No deer I ever shot brought me such joy and exhilaration. The fatherly pride flowed like whitewater rapids.

After retrieving my little deer from the forest edge, roll after roll of film was exposed to save the moment of celebration for all three of us. Now in the expert hands of Mark Ditzel Wildlife Artistry in Hanover, Michigan, the mounted head of this magnificent animal will join the photos and the pretty nine-point Texas buck of his sister and other beautiful game displayed with reverence in our home. The family that hunts together stays together. I love my son, the deerhunter.

CHAPTER 34

MY SON, THE PIGKILLER— HOW PROUD CAN A DAD GET?

WE GOT THE MALLS. We got the video arcades. We got the movie theater complexes. We got the city parks. We got the home video games. We got the big screen TV. We got cartoons, *The Simpsons* and *Fox Kids*. We got the satellite dish. We got the trampoline. We got the dirt bike. We got the four-wheelers. We got guitars and drums. We got canoes and rowboats. We got jet skis. We got dogs, fishing gear, bows and arrows, and we got the guns and ammo. We got the Red Wings, the Lions, and the Tigers. We play little league, roller hockey, ice hockey, gymnastics, karate, and soccer. How all-American can a family get? And how does a mom and

If God didn't want us to eat pork why would He have put all that meat on pigs and deal with their stinking porcine misbehavior on Noah's ark?

dad steer their kids away from the squatmaster activities like video and TV garbage and toward meaningful, quality, educational activities that won't turn them into zombies? It ain't easy, that's for sure. But it *can* be done. Watch me.

First off, we have rules in our home. A certain minimum amount of chores are required daily to establish a well-rounded sense of individual responsibility while assisting in a practical family-oriented team effort. That should be standard in any household. Period. You like dogs and puppies? Shovel, water, and feed. You eat dinner? Let us wash dishes. Cleaning up one's own room, doing laundry, taking out the trash, sweeping, vacuuming, mowing the lawn, raking leaves, and overall general home maintenance should be instilled into a youngster's mind. The discipline is essential, and the sense of self-sufficiency goes a long way to provide a strong base for self-confidence or what some refer to as self-esteem. Either way, a kid will feel incomplete if he or she fails to function in a productive way. Believe it.

No one will ever convince those of us who touch and celebrate God's creation that by any stretch of the imagination the animal rights denial and fantasy is anything but a joke.

Having been raised by a loving mom and dad myself, my brothers and sister and I have turned into reasonably good, law-abiding, upstanding members of our communities, and I am certain that the love in the form of guidance, discipline, and well-organized family activities played essential roles in forming our social and moral compasses.

And there's all that hunting and shooting, too. From the day I could walk, I was out there hunting, shooting, fishing, exploring, and cherishing every waking moment beyond the pavement. Today, I have continued this outdoor heritage with my children, and it has obviously paid off in gargantuan dividends. All my kids have been shooting since they were three or four years old, and the inherent safety and marksmanship disciplines have gone hand in hand with all other basic disciplines to form a strong, independent, goal-oriented mindset in their everyday lives. Makes an old dad glow, dontchya know.

Just today, my wonderful young son Rocco came home with an all "A" report card, a glowing smile, and an itching to shoot his .223 bolt action rifle. He has slowly graduated from air rifle to .22, and now on to centerfire calibers that will be good for taking larger game. We settled in at the range, tacked up some paper bull's-eye targets, set up some old bowling pins, reviewed exacting safety procedures, and loaded up for some fun shooting. Leroy over at The Gun Shop in Quincy, Michigan, set up a nice variable power scope for Rocco on a simple, inexpensive, used Remington 788 in the light recoiling .223 caliber. With ear and eye protectors in place, we commenced to zero-in the small rifle, slow and easy. We rehearsed the breathing, trigger control, and squeeze until Rocco was busting the X ring consistently. He grinned ear to ear. So did Dad.

He was shooting so well that we discussed the need for a family Easter ham coming up and decided we would hunt for a wild hog at Sunrize Acres. Like so many hunting operations in the Midwest, Sunrize offers year round excitement for wild, long-haired, long-tusked, rangy, wild boar, with pure organic, ultra yummy porkmeat attached to their skeletons. If God didn't want us to eat pork why would He have put all that meat on pigs and deal with their stinking porcine misbehavior on Noah's ark? One smoked ham, coming up.

The next day after school Rocco and I once again spent a while at the range further building confidence in boy and gun. In full camo, Rocco was chomping at the bit to get after them hogs because now Mom was relying on us to literally bring home the bacon. Rocco had accompanied me on many different pighunts across the country and witnessed the difficulty in stalking these elusive, wary, ultra spooky wild porkers. He knew it was no sure thing. That's why they call it hunting.

We started out into the wind at the edge of a huge pine grove bordering a cornfield and woodlot. We walked ever so slowly, examining every detail of the wildground we hunted. His eagle eyes showed me the redtail hawk, the distant crows and vultures on their return north, and a continual buzzing of beautiful songbirds all around us. A small group of always fascinating whitetail deer fed along the open hay field at wood's edge, and we knelt to examine tracks, beds, rubs, and old scrapes. Rocco even found two shed antlers and our emotional bag limit was filling up fast.

Just as we eased up a brushy knob of ground, black forms darted away into the distant timber. Even with the strong wind in our face, these alert, wild animals reacted as defensively as Rocky Mountain elk in the National forests of Colorado. This was not going to be easy. It never is.

We sat and rested as a trio of wood ducks took flight from the little waterhole in the woods. A woodpecker hammered a dead sassafras tree above us, and the blue sky let the sunshine warm our backsides. The Great Spirit of the Wild seems even more intense when a father and son share her splendor. We talked quietly about school, guns, animals, girls, Mom's Easter card, and what kind of flowers we should get her. A freeflowing, open, and uninhibited dialogue has always been the reward of quality time spent with my children, and I thank God I was brought up this way. We were having a great day. But now we had to find us a pig, for we had vowed not to buy a store-packaged ham for our Easter dinner table. We either kill our own or go hungry. Back to the chase.

We walked, we stalked, we glassed, we searched, we had fun, but after many hours still no hog. Then we saw a flash of movement far ahead in the puckerbrush tangle of multiflora rose briars and immediately squatted down and made our move. Crawling through the pungent dead leaves of the woods, we made our way to a tumble of large rocks where Rocco extended his Harris bipod to steady his aim *if* that was a hog we had seen, and *if* he presented a shot. Moments before, Rocco had expressed frustration, even desperation, after a long, tiring day of hunting. But now he glowed with enthusiasm and showed excited nervousness getting into the shooting position and form he had practiced so diligently at the range with Dad. We breathed a little hard and waited. And waited. And waited as the adrenaline pumped on. All at once, a beautiful silver and brown wild boar poked out from the thicket at about 65 yards. Without warning Rocco's little .223 barked and the longhaired beast hunched hard when the dust puffed from his shoulder. The boar pivoted in an instant and vanished back into the briar patch and all was silent. Rocco looked up at me and I smiled a thumbs up with a smack on the back and a whispered yet intense, "ATTABOY SON! GOODSHOT!"

We paused to replay the shot and gather ourselves, confidant that the 65-grain softpoint bullet had punched the vitals and pork was ours. Rocco pocketed the lucky .223 case, prepared another round, and we slowly advanced towards our fallen prize. And sure enough, not 20 yards from point of impact lay one gnarly, yet gorgeous, very dead 175-pound Russian boar that would provide the best eating a family could ever ask for. Rocco virtually jumped for joy, thrilled at his hard-earned success, feeling the very powerful sense that one celebrates knowing they have brought delicious, life-giving food to the family table through genuine effort. The kid was on fire. I would have to give him another "A" on his report card for Pigkilling 101. Attsa my boy!

As the spring sun shone down upon the hunters and the wild crows let out their evening roosting calls, harassing the redtail hawk one last time 'til tomorrow, a father and son sat and admired a gift of pure food in an exciting system of self-sufficiency. We took a whole roll of photos, discussed over and over again the charging details of the day's procedures, gutted the hog, and dragged him out of the woods. All these intense scenes will play on in his mind, and mine, forever, and a very special bond was further strengthened this day between a father and son who love each other very much.

I suppose I will let him play a few video games now and then, but I will make that extra effort to encourage and guide him into the great outdoors at every opportunity. The lessons of nature, the lessons of individual accountability, the real life functions he lived and experienced this day afield will go far in developing his independence and understanding that food and life come from somewhere. No one will ever convince those of us who touch and celebrate God's creation that by any stretch of the imagination the animal rights denial and fantasy is anything but a joke. My son knows the truth. Me and Rocco, pigkillers and damn proud.

CHAPTER 35

GUNS AND KIDS

MY NINE-YEAR-OLD Son Rocco sailed wildly across the ice, shaving snowdust with every shimmy of his skateblades. His teammates were equally intense in their attempt to be Red Wing heroes of the frozen puckland. It did this old man much good to cheer on and enjoy the discipline and genuine enthusiasm that is competitive sports. You can see the sparkle in the eyes and actions of these youngsters. There is probably nothing more important in a young person's life than organized challenge, particularly in the form of self-discipline that these team sports represent so well. Having role models

> There is probably nothing more important in a young person's life than organized challenge, particularly in the form of self-discipline.

like the Detroit Red Wings is a blessing all parents
should take advantage of. With but a modicum of
encouragement and prodding, the kids will celebrate the
instinct burning inside them. The physical exercise
alone would do a world of upgrade in a nation with an
embarrassing epidemic of obesity in children. Parents
owe their kids more than that.

But this Saturday would provide a bounty of discipline, fun, challenge, and self-control. For immediately
after early morning ice hockey practice, we loaded up the
family truck with shotguns, ammo, vests, shooting
glasses, and hearing protection, grabbed a bagel and some
orange juice, and headed for what is in my mind the ultimate form of quality family action available anywhere.

At The Gun Shop in Quincy, Michigan, we joined
the Michigan State Police for their annual DARE fund-
raising claybird shoot. As a proud Drug Abuse Resistance
Education officer since the inception of the program, I
was eager to witness once again the powerful, positive
impact such a well-organized shootfest had on so many
young people and their families. All kids are fascinated by
guns, and by participating in this proven National Rifle
Association firearm safety program, these kids would be
part of the team of millions upon millions of youngsters
who safely and responsibly enjoy the shooting sports with
family and friends all across the country. As an NRA lifer

and second-term member of the Board of Directors, I glowed with the knowledge that all these kids were on the True North track.

Joined by dedicated moms, dads, NRA and various gun club members, and law enforcement personnel from nearly every agency, there was a festive spirit in the air, at the range and at the BBQ stand, too. The excitement in all the children's faces bespoke a tale of grand cheer and anticipation. Kids of all ages, from little tots to teenagers, talked and examined each others' guns and shared the enthusiasm that always surrounds such an event. Not a gangbanger, graffiti vandal, dope geek, laughable saggy-pants rapper, or sour-faced punk to be found! Day after day, year after year, these family gatherings take place at exclusive sport clubs, public gun ranges, family farms, state game areas or the local gravel pit without a problem, injury, or disruption. We are talking wild-eyed kids with guns in hand, ammo in their pockets, and not a negligent discharge to be heard of. Wouldn't it be nice if someone in the media would report any of these wholesome, quality family gun events instead of the exclusive coverage they clamor for when a criminal misuse of a firearm takes place? Considering that the lawful, good firearm activity outnumbers the criminal ones by trillions to one, it would seem to be the fair, honest thing to do. Fat chance.

All the eager kids waited their turn and had the time of their lives busting claybirds and improving with every shot. Some were natural athletic marksmen, but everybody had a grand time. Small boys and girls as young as seven blasted away with expert, certified volunteer firearm safety instructors at their side. These cops put their hearts and souls into this knowing full well that this simple, enjoyable, and contagious quality control will go far in the prevention of juvenile delinquent damage control down the road. If the antigun nuts had their way, these proven methods of training would end tomorrow. According to the U.S. Justice Department, more than six thousand kids were caught bringing guns to school between 1996 and 1998, yet only thirteen were prosecuted and *none* were punished. That's a message kids don't miss. Accountability hell. In many of these instances, it was a properly NRA-firearm-program-trained kid who knew what to do and averted tragedy. Like the two faculty members who used their own guns to save lives in Jonestown, Pennsylvania, and Pearl, Mississippi, it was two NRA-trained brothers in Springfield, Oregon, who used their training to subdue a maniac school shooter and end his violent rampage.

Not a gangbanger, graffiti vandal, dopegeek, laughable saggy-pants rapper, or sour faced punk to be found!

Meanwhile pathetic youth with no decent parental direction in Washington, D.C., where firearms ownership is prohibited, go right on shooting each other. What a great idea to implement that policy elsewhere. Crazy. You want to do something about it? Tell Congress: Punish the bad guys with tough, mandatory penalties; and support the good guys—the millions of responsible gun owners—by protecting their vital, God-given, Constitutionally guaranteed, Second Amendment rights. Got it? Good.

We wrapped up the shootfest with everyone in attendance happy and impressed with the day-long event. With hunting season upon us there was much electricity in the air, parents and children alike thrilled to get out there where the pure, natural harvest unfolds. With shooting eyes well-honed, visions of tasty meals sprung to life in most everyone's mind. These families know the truism that if we spend heart and soul time with our kids they'll repay us by being clear-eyed, honest, and responsible. It worked for my mom and dad, all my cousins, and millions of families around the world. It has paid me spiritual dividends with my wonderful children. I guarantee it will work for you. The alternatives are not pretty.

CHAPTER 36

NUGE'S MESSAGE TO KIDS

NOTHING IS MORE important than getting the message out to kids: to get high on life not high on drugs, to enjoy God's creation, to use their God-given intelligence and spirit— NOT to zone out like a fattening couch-potato and NOT to pound their brains to mush with the peer-pressured poison du jour. When I get kids together at my Ted Nugent Kamp for Kids or other kid-friendly gatherings, I give them the full-metal gospel— something like this...

> I will say "No, thank you" once, then the feisty guitarboy comes out swinging.

Greetings to my fine Spirit of the Wild youthful BloodBrothers all! Do not think for one all American workin' hard, playin' hard, rockin' hard, huntin' hard, shootin' hard, livin' strong minute that I don't think of all you young Americans every wild day of my adventurous life. Like all of our Ted Nugent United Sportsmen of America members and dedicated Ted Nugent Kamp for Kids volunteers, Tribe Nuge cares deeply about all of you, heart and soul. As I slam on with *year fifty-two* of my stimulating rock 'n' roll fun and games, touring like a Madman on a mission, I wish to share some simple observations based on actual hand-to-hand combat first-person experiences that drive my magnum fun-filled life. And by God, you little monkeys know that ol' Hunka Ted is indeed having a Gonzo load of fun! YOWSA and pass the Spirit!

How, ask ye, does an old fart like that historical goofball Nuge have so much dangtootin' fun and be in total control of his adventurous life? Memorize this, kids—write it down, and spread it as far and wide as you possibly can. Ready? I CELEBRATE EACH AND EVERY DAY OF MY JOYOUS LIFE WITH SUCH INTENSITY BECAUSE I AM FIFTY-TWO YEARS CLEAN AND SOBER!

Got that? The old boy is absolutely on fire! No drugs, no alcohol, no tobacco, no poison, no BS! No idiots getting me to buy into any numbnut peer pressure—NO WAY! Peer pressure is for stupid sheep. And ya know what sheep do don't ya? They mindlessly wander around like lost jerks and stick their sheepy nose up some other sheep's butt and follow them around with no direction of their own. In other words, they got no life. They got no spirit. They got no attitude. They got no nothin'. How worthless could a life be? Peer pressure can kiss my ass.

Here's what drives every day of my life. Say it loud and proud! I AM IN CHARGE OF MY LIFE, THANK YOU! Anybody who tries to get me to do something stupid like taking drugs, drinking booze, touching any tobacco slop, sniffin' paint, huffin' anything except good fresh air, breaking the law, painting graffiti, being rude, causing trouble, shoplifting, eating junk, eating too much, making a stupid decision, piercing a body part, tattooin' my flesh, or eating a broken glass sandwich had best get outta my way. What kind of fools do they think we are? I will say "No, thank you" once, then the feisty guitarboy comes out swinging. That's right kids, I believe in fighting for what you believe in. After all, an offer to poison yourself is an offer to destroy your life, even kill you. That's a serious threat where I come from.

So get tough and don't take any crap from anyone. This is war, my friends. A war for your lives and your quality of life for sure. The amount of fun and happiness you get out of each day will be determined by how smart you are in deciding right over wrong, FOR YOUR-

SELF. You will have guaranteed fun, be happy, feel in control, and make your family proud! Now THAT'S living kids! Believe me, I know.

I know that sometimes you feel unsure of yourselves; sometimes we all get confused and wonder. Me, too! Sometimes everybody is so busy that you feel alone. Well, here's what you young warriors oughtta do. Go up to mom and dad, big brother, big sister, your favorite aunt or uncle, or grandma or grandpa, and ask them for a little time. PLEASE! Get pushy. Because I know they love you and want to get better time together just as much as you do, but sometimes in this crazy world many people get carried away with work and other responsibilities. But you kids can actually help them help you. Before you go to bed at night tell mom and dad just what you are feeling. Tell them you want to do something fun next weekend. Tell them you would love to go into the beautiful forests and wildgrounds of our great nation. Tell them you would love to learn to safely shoot a .22 rifle or a bow and arrow. Tell them you would love to learn about birdsongs and wild animal tracks. Tell them you want to feel the Spirit of the Wild. Tell them ya wanna GO WILD! Because the more time I spend in the wild, the better I feel. The more sure I am of myself, the more fun I have. The discipline of firearm and archery marksmanship will help you in everything you do.

Because discipline will help you focus on a higher quality of life that is special here in the good old U.S. of A.

And take a camera with you so you can share the beauty and adventure of your wonderful outdoor family experiences. As you show your friends these pictures I bet you can convince them to join you in your next outdoor maneuver. And I bet you anything that you will all learn to make better decisions in your life that will bring you more FUN and HAPPINESS! In fact, I promise you it will. That's where I have gotten all of my energy, attitude, and spirit for nearly fifty-two years so far, and I know it is where I still get it more and more every year.

So take a tip from ol' Hunka Ted. GO WILD and have the time of your life. Spread that excitement with all your family and friends and know that I am with you every time you feel the Great Spirit. Godbless, Godspeed, and live it up. I love y'all, BloodBrothers, Hunka Hunka Burnin' Ted. 🏹

CHAPTER 37

FRED BEAR AND BEYOND

"THERE I WAS back in the wild again. I felt right
at home, where I belong. I had that feeling coming over
me again, just like it happened so many times before.

The spirit of the woods is like an old good
friend. Makes me feel warm and good inside. I know
his name, it's good to see him again. Cuz in the wind
he's still alive.

Fred Bear, walk with me down the trails again.
Take me back, back where I belong. Fred Bear, I'm
glad to have you at my side my friend, and I'll join you
in the big hunt before too long.

It was kind of dark, another misty dusk. It came
from the tangle down below. I tried to remember
everything he taught me so well, I had to decide which
way to go.

Was I alone, or in a hunter's dream? The
moment of truth is here and now. I felt his touch, I felt
his guiding hand, and the buck was mine forever
more.

Fred Bear walks with me down those trails
again. He takes me back, back where I belong. Fred
Bear, I'm glad to have you at my side my friend, and
I'll join you in the big hunt before too long.

We're not alone when we're in the great outdoors. We got his spirit, we got his soul. He will guide
our steps, he will guide our arrows home. The restless
spirit forever roams.

In the wind, he's still alive."

Those lyrics came gushing forth on a cool spring
morning in 1989. Fred Bear had passed away just a year
earlier, on April 8, 1988. My wonderful mother had just
recently died as well, and the emotions came on like a
torrent. A haunting arpeggio guitar lick had played itself
the night before in a rather appropriate setting, deep in
the beautiful wilds of the Manistee National Forest in
our stunning northern cabin on the sparkling, big,
timber-framed lake. Surrounded by my loving family, I
had picked a few riffs on my guitar as the sun went down
following a grand day of fishing and wilderness adventure with my children, wife, and her family. Spirits were

running high, to say the least, and in the glow of a crackling, warming fire, the guitar seemed to take on a life of its own—as is usually the case when ideas flourish. I did not relate the interesting chord pattern to anything special, but I did know that it was indeed special. We loaded up the truck and headed home with bellies full of delicious fresh bluegill and bass filets and a special feeling that always comes from time together at the cabin.

I had to overcome and correct his mistaken stereotype that all rock 'n' rollers were drug infested, antihunting pukes destroying America.

With the kids back in school the next morning and the farm routine back into gear, I had just finished running the dogs and doing my morning chores when I went to grab the bow and arrows for my morning shoot. But as I was about to walk out of the house, bow in hand, I stopped myself for no apparent reason, set down the bow, and walked back into the living room and picked up the guitar. A race between sobbing tears and intense guitar licks erupted, the likes of which I had never before experienced. I sobbed and literally gasped to such a degree that Shemane rushed into the room to see if I had seriously injured myself, and I continuted to cry in her bosom for the longest time. She consoled me as I stammered out words of love and sadness about Fred, not being able to stop myself. Shemane held me tight in her arms and encouraged me to pursue my inspiration. I felt driven to discover these powerful emotions through this unstoppable musical tribute to Fred, and the lyrics flowed as if I had sung this new song a million times before. It was quite eerie. Struggling to gather myself from my current state of emotional wreckage, I wrote down the words and sang them over and over again. After about an hour I stopped sobbing enough to speak, and I immediately called Henrietta, Fred's widow, to share with her what I knew would be a piece of music that would touch her like it was touching me. I set the phone on the table before me, and milking blood from my acoustic guitar, and with much difficulty, I sang the new composition to her. She, too, turned to jelly. We cried together and talked for a long time that morning, and she made me promise her I would record the song and send her a tape right away.

Fortunately, my ace rhythm section, bass guitarist Michael Lutz and drummer Gunner Ross, could make an emergency session the next morning at Pearl Sound in Canton, Michigan. The studio was available for only a brief two-hour opening early that morning, and owner Ben Gross would help with engineering and production duties. My goal here was to merely capture the basic arrangement for Henrietta's and my own personal listening. We set up what amplifiers and gear that happened to be there for a basic makeshift recording session and let 'er rip. To say that magic was in the air that cloudy morning would be a monstrous understatement, for Michael and Gunner dove headfirst into the spirit of my emotional contact with Fred and a truly mystical aura winged freely throughout the short session. It was a wonderful mood.

Upon completion of a single run-through to teach the guys the arrangement, we nailed it in the first take, accurately capturing the essence of my love for the man and the spiritual impact his lessons of nature had and continues to have on my life.

Not only was the performance intense and spirited, but of equal dynamic was the incredible detailed blend attained with our hurried mixing of the tracks. What was at the time but a hopeful quick reference tape was turning into a moving piece of classic Nuge music. I had no thoughts whatsoever of any commercial use for the song. We let the music steer the entire morning, and we felt the magic. We scurried to fetch an old 1964 LP of Fred conducting an interview with Curt Gowdy of the ABC television show *American Sportsman* in order to lift some of Fred's own words for a possible inclusion somewhere on my recording. It all came together as if guided by a hand from above. As we rode the faders,

Ben on the drum tracks, Michael on the vocals, and my hands clutching the lead vocal and guitar tracks, we mixed the song by the seat of our pants. As the lead guitar track augmented the outchorus into a soulful frenzy, amazingly my random feedback sounds perfectly coincided with my ad-lib scat style lead vocal improvisations. For example, having never performed much less recorded the song before (it was less than a day old), I could not have known I would mention the word "swamp" in the final outchorus, but as I did, the Paul Reed Smith guitar, which is not known for its feedback capabilities, hummed a swamplike feedback note, perfectly answering the word. When I ad-libbed during the last chorus and spontaneously said, "Fred, talk to me," we inserted Fred's own voice from his recording as he said, "If today's teenage thrillseekers really want to get a thrill, let them go up into the Northwest and tangle with a grizzly bear, a polar bear, or a brown bear, they will get a thrill that will cleanse the soul." Everyone looked at each other in disbelief, feeling the chills that come only when unexplained events unfold under such miraculous conditions. It was very exciting.

I sent the rough mix to Henrietta, and I played mine for some old hunting buddies who knew and respected Fred. Old George Nicholls and John Kalash both came to tears and asked for a copy. My huntin' buddy and a genuine fan of Fred's, Bob Blevins, also had to have one, so I made about a dozen cassettes because Henrietta wanted more for family and friends. Then it happened. Someone, to this day I don't know who, snuck a cassette to Doug Podell at WLLZ rock radio in Detroit and all hell broke loose. To make a long story short, the requests haven't stopped yet, and eleven years later the "Fred Bear" song remains one of the all-time most requested songs on every rock station in Michigan and some areas of Wisconsin and Pennsylvania, and hundreds of thousands of recordings have been sold at sporting goods stores and through mail order. My live performances of the song are chilling and have to be seen and heard to be believed. People go ballistic with joy and celebration of Fred and the Spirit of the Wild. It is embraced as the official hunter's theme song by all who have heard it, and the testimonies from across the land emphasize its influence far and wide. I could not be more proud.

My first encounter with the great man was in early October, probably around 1952 or thereabouts. I was only four years old. My greatest fortune in life remains the fact that my dad was already one of the visionary pioneers of this renewed interest in the art of bowhunting, and with Fred Bear leading the charge out of Grayling, Michigan, most archers made it a point to stop at his new, one-room archery shop on their way north during the early bow and arrow deer season. In those first years on our family's annual trips Up North, I was surely too young to grasp the dynamics at hand, but there is no doubt that I was being imprinted with what would surely become the most powerful force in my life: the mystical flight of the arrow and all associated discipline therein! After but just a few years in the deerwoods, it wasn't long before I became aware of this special man's special touch with nature and his clever marketing skills. He was to forever be a growing force and guidance in all aspects of my life.

Inspired by the exploits of Doctors Saxton Pope and Arthur Young, Fred discovered an exciting upgrade in his pursuit of the wild in the close-range demands of the bow and arrow as a big game hunting tool. Pope and Young became infatuated with the Spirit of the Wild after studying the last Indian of the Yani tribe discovered in Northern California at the turn of the Twentieth Century. Amazed at Ishi's mystical connection with nature and deft touch as a bowhunter, Pope and Young began filming their experiments with archery equipment, and made several awe-inspiring films of their hunts in Alaska and Africa. Witnessing these thrilling adventures on the local movie theater newsreels in Detroit around 1925, Fred plunged headfirst into the flight of the arrow and the stimulating world of bowhunting. A lifelong rifle hunter,

Fred was intensely intrigued by what appeared to be the insurmountable challenge of getting close enough to kill large game with the bow and arrow. In the face of the industrial revolution's mindset of "easier is better," a hardcore tribe of dedicated, self-sufficient, rugged individuals were looking for just the opposite—deeper gratification from a more demanding challenge. The fire had been lit. Fred became a dedicated bowhunter, and later, once he had mastered it himself, he became an evangelist for the sport.

Fred began a promotional blitzkrieg on major TV, radio, and print media. Always the gentleman, he extolled the virtues of conservation and the healing powers of nature with down-to-earth, hands-on believability. He emphasized ethics, safety, and respect for wildlife through a creed of sportsmanship that he lived. His style was endearing, and his pleasant demeanor attracted young and old, male and female alike. I, for one, was absolutely mesmerized by his overall presence and looked forward to each fall's visit in Grayling. The hunting community could not have asked for a better ambassador than Fred Bear.

By the age of five or six, I was already addicted to wildlife and the wildground that seemed to call my name. Living across the street from the wild edges of Detroit's suburban Redford Township, I couldn't get enough of stalking the woodlands and wetlands of the Rouge River watercourse that wound deeply through the patchwork of forests adjacent to our home at 23251 Florence near the intersection of Hazelton. Skunk Hollow was a marshy area within the bend of the stinky, polluted Rouge, and I would explore there nearly every day. While all the other kids were playing ballgames, I was sneaking through the nastiest thickets I could find, slowly learning the ultimate lessons in cause-and-effect accountability. My best hunting buddy, cousin Mark Schmitt, was my companion on many of these adventures, and we struck a bond that lives on to this day.

The cycle of life and death is not flexible. We have no right to an opinion of it. It just plain is.

We learned more valuable lessons in responsibility and teamwork than could ever be gleaned from a textbook or formal education process. The term BloodBrothers struck a nerve, and the world would be a much better place if more people sought that deep, heart-and-soul connection with each other and the good Mother Earth that gives us life and joy. Even the lowly river rats would intrigue us, teaching us to move slowly, carefully placing each step like it mattered. And if we paid attention, we could get to fulldraw on our little longbows and sink a cedar arrow through their body, pinning them to the bank. Conversely, when I was not quite alert enough they scurried away as every custom-designed, defense-oriented beast has done for time immemorial. All the defenseless animals are long gone.

My dad, in many ways, taught me this, but in the final analysis it was the genius of Fred Bear combined with his innate gregarious nature that really struck a chord with millions of us looking for the ultimate contact with our inner soul. Self-sufficiency and total independence are no better exemplified than by the act of procuring one's own sustenance. And though a firearm would be far more efficient, in the days of exploding conservation awareness, game populations likewise exploded and hunting opportunities ascended accordingly. Though one's success at hunting would not ultimately translate into a life-and-death determination, it is the desire to be in charge of one's own destiny that will indeed determine one's confidence in quality of life control. I am proud to celebrate that the Nugent family has not partaken in store-bought flesh in over thirty years. The mere fact that zero cases of E.coli or salmonella have ever been found in any wildgame meat is testimony enough to the deep and abiding respect hunters have for our game, both on the hoof and on the dinner plate. You see, when we go to all that gargantuan effort to return to our predatorship, hone our marksmanship and hunting skills, learn the way of the wild, and ultimately maximize our time in the presence of always fascinating wildlife, there is no way in hell we are going to let this hard-earned prize go bad or be tainted in any way.

Like the aboriginal tribes, the proud Native American hunters, and African warriors, we cherish the productivity of the good Mother Earth and cannot imagine anything but reverence for her offerings. This is what Fred Bear taught me.

He taught me for many years. Our encounters in Grayling at Bear Archery and the Grayling Restaurant were special for me and my family. But it wasn't until I graduated from high school in '67 and returned to Michigan that I really got to know Fred one on one. And that was no easy task, as I had to overcome and correct his mistaken stereotype that all rock 'n' rollers were drug infested, antihunting pukes destroying America. That was not accomplished very quickly, but over the years, his staff and company workers would excitedly explain to him how militantly antidrug and adamantly proconservation and prohunting I was. By the early 1970s he and his wonderful wife Henrietta regularly invited me into their home and treated me like family. I was beside myself with joy. To sit in Fred's personal home archery test shop and fondle tomorrow's archery ideas was a high point for this old arrow-flinging rockin' doggy. I would sit there, listen to his stories, examine his newest invention, dry fire his custom hammerless 5-inch Smith & Wesson M29 .44 magnum, and do everything in my power not to drool all over myself.

Eventually, Fred invited me to hunt with him in Alaska and elsewhere. I joined him for many memorable hunts at his private Grouse Haven Lodge outside Rose City, Michigan, and cherished every moment. Sitting around the fireplace at the end of each day's activities and listening to Fred and Bob Munger retell wild and exotic hunt tales was a dream come true. These guys were witty, clever story weavers, and they really conveyed a dynamic sense of uninhibited adventure. Sometimes more uninhibited than anyone might have believed. It was always fascinating, and I felt privileged to be included. I will never forget a minute of these times—especially our last intimate dialogue together in mid October 1987. When all the other hunters were out in their treestands, Fred and I went for a little stroll together under a beautiful blue-grey autumn sky within the canopy of flamethrowing hardwoods. The maples were a firestorm of reds, oranges, yellows, and golds; the beech a deep, dark gold; and the black, white, and red oaks were varying shades of rust, red, and orange. Overhead skeins of waterfowl punctuated the hunter's calm, and Fred and I just walked and talked. He

All the defenseless animals are long gone.

had his ever-present oxygen bottle over his left shoulder and his right hand on my arm. His words of encouragement that day became a guiding force in the formation of my Ted Nugent Kamp for Kids when he told me to continue promoting archery, conservation, hunting, and the shooting sports as I had been, connecting with America's youth via the rock 'n' roll vehicle. He encouraged me to ignore my critics' squawking, that he had endured the same nonsense as he took on the leadership of bowhunting, and that the hunting industry and community were loaded with a disproportionate number of unsophisticated, pompous bastards who lived to complain and point fingers at anyone who succeeds. With the resistance I had encountered heretofore at the hands of such people, Fred's motivating words came at a crucial time for me. I took them to heart.

With eyes agog, I would take it all in like a human sponge, appreciating and cataloging his every word. I can close my eyes and see him any time I wish. When I sing his song, it is best I don't close my eyes and see him, for it is so emotional that the words and memories overwhelm me and I become a sobbing lump of trembling, uncontrollable tears. He means that much to me. Watch me someday if you are at one of my concerts, and see my eyes well up and the veins on my forehead and forearms pulsate with every word. It is as if he is there with us. For he is.

I take to heart how his song has connected with so many. Since writing the song upon his death, I have received volumes of correspondence from people across America on how it has touched their lives. Many have stated that it has triumphantly changed their lives for the better. Fathers and sons exclaim how it has brought them together. Fighting brothers boast of it bringing them back together for the hunt. It is played on opening days, at birthdays, graduations, bar mitzvahs, weddings, funerals, and every celebration known to man. For this I am extremely thankful. In the wind, he's still alive.

As I leave the pavement each fall, bow in hand, I am learning to take it a little slower, a bit more conscientiously, dedicated to increase my attentiveness and level of awareness in order to maximize the overall spiritual experience. Discipline at its finest. Fred is with me, so is Dad, Uncle John, George, and so many other campfire friends. I call them BloodBrothers, for our relationship remains the essence of being alive, celebrating the truth of nature's laws, tooth, fang, and claw, in all her glory, and the thoughtful men who opened the doors to the wild and all its stimuli. The bond is eternal.

The cycle of life and death is not flexible. We have no right to an opinion of it. It just plain is. Her force is more powerful than convenient supposition. Animals cannot have rights, as the very precept is a notion of man's. Animals, like man, rather, have a role in this unforgivable cycle. Those species with the capability of logic, reason, and forethought will do better when applying these beneficial powers. Those limited to instincts and a fight-or-flight response will do just fine as well, most of the time. But the power to reason remains the dividing line between man and beast, and where man fails to give this select talent due consideration, he is doomed to his self-inflicted morass of denial and its inescapable plight of failure. Survival of the fittest is as it should be. Not the current hell of "thriving of the sickest" as we see more and more often in the imbalanced world of modern man today. Accountability must have its rewards and punishments. Where we find rampant recidivism, we witness the code of man shattered and skewered. Where we fail to respond with sense and reason, we watch sense and reason vanish from the equation. That is the saddest disservice we provide our youth. If the dog begs at the dinner table and we allow it, we actually create it. Don't blame the dog if he ends up in our soup bowl. We get what we ask for.

How much more control are we willing to forsake? How many more random acts of violence are we going to feign shock at? How many more times are we going to cower under tables and chairs, whimpering like mindless dogs, thinking that someone else has the responsibility to save and protect us? How much further are we willing to allow our souls to erode in a tailspin of dependency? When is it appropriate to hide, whimper, and cry? I say never! To accept laws that ensure helplessness is pathetic. Some may ask me if I believe we are ready for an armed society. I say damn straight. Only those who believe their lives worth protecting and saving should venture forth armed. The rest can hope for a miracle. I, for one, keep my radar on red alert at all times. Not to the point anywhere near paranoia, but rather the desirable condition of relaxed preparedness for the simple reason that I don't want to miss anything. Not just poised for danger, but 100 percent eager to live to the fullest all fun, interesting, joyful opportunities as they unfold and surface before me. I like a good groove, but the only rut I allow indulgence in is the breeding season of herbivorous critters. I like when sparks fly. Now that's my kind of rut. I will be there for as long as I can possibly eke out a meaningful role therein. I'll be the tall guy with the predator grin, an erect ponytail, and the middle fingers on perpetual standby. Cocked, locked, and ready to rock, doc. I AM the damned mystical flight of the eternal arrow. Watch me. Join me. In the Spirit of the Wild. 🏹

[THANX LIST]

MY SOARING QUALITY OF LIFE is possible only for the teamwork of those gifted individuals who have dedicated themselves for so many years. Here I will attempt a comprehensive list to salute them all:

I thank and salute Doug Banker, Bob Quandt, Fred Bear, Linda Peterson, Charlton Heston, Kirk Gibson, Jim Lawson, Wayne LaPierre, Kathy Valdez, Connie Nelson, Bob Munger, Elmer Kieth, Ward Parker, Lee Fields, Dennis Arfa, John Kolodner, Pablo Gamboa, Erica Rogers, Gwen Nappi, Harry Crocker, Al Regnery, Marja Walker, Tommy Aldridge, Marco Mendoza, Kayne Robinson, Johnny Gunnel, Derek St. Holmes, Jack and Molly Blades, Steve Fortney, the Nallis, Jim Curnutt, Michael Cartellone, Tommy Shaw, John Rocker, Joe Vitale, Johnny Angelos, Rob Rusga, Michael Lutz, Benny Rappa, Gunnar Ross, Gary Hicks, Bob Lehnert, Gale Uptadale, Dick Treat, Andy Solomon, Dave Palmer, Dave Amato, Gabe Magno, Tony Reale, Lew Futterman, Tom Werman, Charlie Huhn, Craig Colburn, John Conk, Jimmy Douglas, Jimmy Johnson, Mark Newman, Dan Beck, Doug Morris, David Krebs, Carmine Appice, Vic Mastrianni, Todd Howarth, Greg Arama, John Brake and family, John Finly, Tom Noel,

Pete Prim, Pete DeYoung, Steve Farmer, K.J. Knight, Cliff Davies, Steve Brown, Rob DeLaGrange, Bill White, Rick Lober, Keith Johnstone, Mark Ditzel, Bob Blevins, Dean Mitchell, Bill "Rip" Mayes, Calvin and Melissa Ross, Steve Sinden, Eric Web, Tony Dukes, Ronnie Bradford, Tim Hart, Bob Hilts, Greg Price, Toby Francis, Jim Yakabuski, NiteBob, Bobby "OD" Oberdorsen, Willy Twork, Mark Vanderwall, Scooter Davis, Laura Kaufman, Mitch Snyder, Earl Miles, Bob Foulkrod, Scott Young, Larry and Celeste Pollack, Jack Brittingham and family, Dan and Kathy Countiss, Clint Starling, Chester Moore, Ken Moody and family, Mike Sohm, Steve and Greg Sims, Frank Mitchell, Mike Hoban, Larry Pratt, Paul Wilson, Bryan Schupbach, Tracy Powell, Chuck Buzzy, Louie, Randy and Cheryl Krick, Rod Peterson, Tom Minsel, Chip Stewart and family, Keith Baker, Brad Landwerlen, Phillip Carter, Kevin Kelly, David Allen, Jason Zins, Mike Kitner, Kevin Smart, Jim McCullough, Robin Stibb, Corey Graff, Richard Putman, Don Gilhousen, Roy Mayer, Lee Welborn, Steve Gelakoski, Fred Ickes, Jon Barnett, Davis Allen, Bill Sheg, Corey Osorio, Tom Polcholski and family, John Feldman, Barry Swanson, Bruce Cull, Scott Asse, Allen Reynolds, Michael Link, Craig Hicks, Joe Vermeulen, Andy Kowalchewski, Ray Gosselin, Gary Fales, Robert Owens, Mike Potts, Pat Durkin, Bill Vaznis, Mike Strandlund, Jim Knight, Bill Parker, Bob Whitehead, Steve Jones, M.R. and

Janet James, John Zent, Jeff Copeland, Jim Williams, Joe Bell, Tom Campbell, Dean Bortz, Thomas Pigeon, Richard P. Smith, Ben Case, Mike Zelinski, Bruce McLaughlin, Kim Hicks, the Schreiners and the Y.O. Ranch family, Bobby Hale, Slayton White, Rush Limbaugh, Ken Hamblin, Mitch Albom, Mark Scott, Mark Davis, Allen Handleman, Rick Lewis, Michael Floorwax, Jaz McCay, Steve Black, Bob Bauer, Joe Bevelaqua, Ken and Kathryn Nass, Suzanne and Steve Magnetta, Cecelia and John Rogers, Todd Albaugh, Angela Kline, Paul Milone, Ed Chadwick, Shelly Griffis, Mike Stumiller, Mike Verdick, Bobby Chiounard, James Brown, Chuck Berry, Shantell Coats-Burns, Tony Dukes, Bernie Goetz, Mas Ayoob, Ken Kelly and Mag-Na-Port Arms, Marv Leslie, Browning, Peter Pi and Cor-Bon, Ruger, Colt, Roy Jinks and S&W, Winchester, Remington, Dwight VanBrunt and Kimber, Black Hills Ammunition, Fiochi, Martin Archery, Glock, Mossy Oak, the Galco family, Clif Cook and Michaels of Oregon, Carlos Santiago and USA Mags, Sean Craddock of HK, all our Ted Nugent Kamp for Kids volunteers and graduates, and all those extremely dedicated workin' hard, playin' hard, rock 'n' roll Americans and radio and media people all around the world who have supported and provided a format to me for so many years, Godbless, Godspeed, and hammer on True North. ⚔

[RESOURCES]

FOR INFORMATION ON Ted Nugent United Sportsmen of America and *Ted Nugent Adventure Outdoors Magazine*, or to receive a free Ted Nugent catalog, call or write: P.O. Box 220, Concord, MI 49237, 800-343-HUNT. For information on the Ted Nugent Kamp for Kids, call or write P.O. Box 532, Concord, MI 49237, 517-750-KAMP. To book personalized hunts with Ted Nugent, call or write Sunrize Safaris, P.O. Box 220, Concord, MI 49237, 800-343-HUNT. And visit our web site: www.tnugent.com or TedNugent.com.